W9-CFB-748

One-Pot Chocolate Desserts

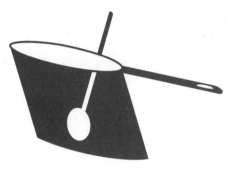

BROADWAY BOOKS · NEW YORK

One-Pot Chocolate Desserts

50 Recipes for Making
Chocolate Desserts from
Scratch, Using a Pot,
a Spoon, and a Pan

Andrew Schloss

with Ken Bookman

To Erika and Michael

BROADWAY

ONE-POT CHOCOLATE DESSERTS. Copyright © 1997 by Andrew Schloss with Ken Bookman. All rights reserved. Printed in the United States of America. No part of this book may be reproduced or transmitted in any form or by any means, electronic or mechanical, including photocopying, recording, or by any information storage and retrieval system, without written permission from the publisher. For information, address Broadway Books, a division of Bantam Doubleday Dell Publishing Group, Inc., 1540 Broadway, New York, NY 10036.

Broadway Books titles may be purchased for business or promotional use or for special sales. For information, please write to: Special Markets Department, Bantam Doubleday Dell Publishing Group, Inc., 1540 Broadway, New York, NY 10036.

BROADWAY BOOKS and its logo, a letter B bisected on the diagonal, are trademarks of Broadway Books, a division of Bantam Doubleday Dell Publishing Group, Inc.

Library of Congress Cataloging-in-Publication Data
Schloss, Andrew, 1951–
    One-pot chocolate desserts : 50 recipes for making chocolate desserts from scratch, using a pot, a spoon, and a pan / Andrew Schloss with Ken Bookman. — 1st ed.
        p.   cm.
    Includes index.
    ISBN 0-7679-0084-7 (hardcover)
    1. Cookery (Chocolate) 2. Desserts. 3. Quick and easy cookery. I. Bookman, Ken. II. Title.
    TX767.C5S36   1997
    641.6'374—dc21   97-14810
                                                      CIP

FIRST EDITION

Designed by Debbie Glasserman

97 98 99 00 01 10 9 8 7 6 5 4 3 2 1

Contents

Acknowledgments

Our heartfelt thanks go to some people who have been with us before, notably our agent, Judith Weber, and our editor at Broadway Books, Harriet Bell. Some key contributors to this volume are newcomers and we'd like to thank them, too, for their help and input. They include our copyeditor, Sonia Greenbaum; the designer of this volume, Debbie Glasserman; and a most talented photographer, Beatriz Da Costa.

Introduction

I am a klutz.

Yes, I *can* walk and chew gum at the same time, but don't push much beyond that. So what am I doing testing a dessert cookbook? Doesn't making desserts demand some level of flair and dexterity? Good questions, and for the best answers, I go back to something that totally changed my life: Andrew Schloss's and my first dessert cookbook, *One-Pot Cakes: 60 Recipes for Cakes from Scratch Using a Pot, a Spoon, and a Pan.*

Before the one-pot method changed the way I made desserts, I always had the uneasy feeling that my love of desserts, my respect for following the directions of someone who knows a subject better than I, and my caring for good ingredients somehow weren't quite enough. Like, if making a dessert takes less than three hours and doesn't dirty everything in my cupboard, I won't get the full credit. I might as well go to a bakery and buy a *real* dessert.

Guess what? That's nonsense. Part of declaring it nonsense may have to do with my getting older and realizing that life is too short to pretend that I'm good at something I'm not. Part of it, too, is being presented with an alternative—one that tastes wonderful, respects quality ingredients, but also respects my time.

Since the moment that Andy brought the one-pot method into my life, my outlook on desserts has changed. Now a homemade dessert can be an anytime thing, suitable for closing any meal, whether it's a weeknight quickie or a weekend dinner party.

One-Pot Cakes rewarded me with a very special moment. It came shortly after I put the manuscript in the hands of an old friend, a woman of many talents, none of which is cooking. I remember her phone call to me after she made one of the one-pot cakes. I had never heard her voice so animated. And the sheer triumph in her words—the "I-actually-cooked-something-and-it-tastes-great" lilt—told me that this book was for her and for me.

And for you, too.

Let's face it. The dessert geniuses of the world are far fewer in number than the rest of us. So when Andy, my food colleague and longtime cookbook collaborator, came up with dozens of recipes using the one-pot method with the title *One-Pot Cakes*, it was an easy sell. It wouldn't be hard to convince anyone who has ever finished baking a cake and taken note of the kitchen detritus that resulted to buy a cake book that promised a quick three- or four-item cleanup.

But I've always believed that speed and ease constitute only the first hurdle in getting a recipe into the home cook's repertoire. It's the taste that will take it the rest of the way. That has always been Andy's strong suit. He and I have worked together for fifteen years, and while I've always been impressed with his knowledge of how ingredients behave in the kitchen, my deeper awe has been reserved for his sense of how ingredients taste in the finished dish. Quick recipes place an extra flavor burden on every ingredient. The secret to the wonderful taste of the one-pot cakes is his use of what I like to call power ingredients. In *One-Pot Chocolate Desserts*, that means the zests and fruits and extracts that work with the more obvious chocolates and nuts to produce desserts that just flat-out taste great.

One-Pot Cakes was so revolutionary that it didn't take a big leap of logic to extend the concept to this book. Cakes—along with brownies, custards, puddings, and snacks—will all be found in these pages, and they all have two things in common. The first is chocolate, a flavor that has long captivated the American palate. And the second is the one-pot method, a technique you'll learn to do on the spur of the moment, guaranteeing that the recipe will be used, not just imagined.

Ken Bookman
April 1997

How to Use This Book

The love of chocolate is acute. It starts with an innocent Hershey's kiss, and before long you're in the throes of full-blown Valrhona addiction. There has to be something transcendent about a substance that hooks toddlers with a single sip of chocolate milk and doesn't trigger a twelve-step backlash from their double chocolate–chunked parents.

I thought that putting together this book of chocolate desserts might act as a purge for me, but it hasn't. It has only made my dependency deeper, taking it from one-pot chocolate cakes and icings to puddings, custards, brownies, and candies.

If you're familiar with our first one-pot dessert book, *One-Pot Cakes,* you already know how the one-pot method streamlines traditional cake-baking by making it simple enough that it can become an everyday, spur-of-the-moment activity.

One-Pot Chocolate Desserts applies the same principles to desserts that weren't covered in *One-Pot Cakes*—chocolate cookies, brownies, tortes, cheesecakes, puddings, custards, and confections.

To review those one-pot principles:

- The sifting of dry ingredients is streamlined. There's only one reason to sift flour, and that's to aerate it. But aerating flour is essential only for the most delicate sponge or angel food cakes.

- The creaming of butter and sugar is simplified as well. Butter is partially melted in a large saucepan. The heat generated completes the melting off the stovetop. When chocolate is part of the recipe it, too, finishes melting off the heat, along with the butter, so there is no danger of scorching.
- Less heat-sensitive ingredients—sugar, vanilla, spices, and sour cream or yogurt—are added even before the eggs go in. The eggs are added, after the mixture cools to prevent curdling, and then the dry ingredients.
- Baking powder and baking soda are added in pinches to eliminate any lumps before they go into the batter and so they can soften and disperse through the liquid before more dry ingredients get in the way.

In short, the one-pot method gives you the quality of a cake made from scratch with the convenience of a mix—and with less cleanup.

Certainly, there are some desserts (pies, for example) that can't be made from scratch in a single vessel, but you will be amazed at the variety and quality of those that can be made with just one pot, a spoon, and a baking pan. For proof, just look at the two-tone Black and White Almond Ring on page 19, or the quintessential chocolate birthday cake, the Chocolate Buttermilk Layer Cake on page 12.

About Chocolate

Although using chocolate is an effortless way to bake in richness, working with it has its quirks. The first quirk comes when you melt it. Chocolate burns easily, which is why most cookbooks warn against melting chocolate without the protection of a double boiler or a cautiously programmed microwave oven. As mentioned earlier, the one-pot method improves on tradition by avoiding the nuisance of a double boiler and the danger of direct heat by melting chocolate off the stove and right in the pot in which the batter will be mixed.

One-Pot Chocolate Desserts

Most of the recipes in these pages start by adding chocolate to hot melted butter, then stirring so the residual heat from the butter melts the chocolate. That avoids any chance of burning the chocolate and gives the butter enough time to cool to keep it from damaging other heat-sensitive ingredients, like eggs.

Once melted, chocolate can become grainy if it is mixed with water or anything containing water, such as an egg or a liquid flavoring. Since chocolate is an emulsion of water (chocolate liquor) in fat (cocoa butter), adding any additional liquid throws the proportion of ingredients out of whack, breaking the emulsion and leaving behind grains of chocolate in a sea of melted fat. The one-pot method guards against this mishap. Because most one-pot recipes start by melting chocolate with butter, extra liquid can easily be absorbed without causing graininess.

The recipes in this book were tested with Baker's, Nestlé, and Hershey's chocolates—the most commonly available brands. I have used them interchangeably for many years with universally excellent results. You can also find some very fine (and very expensive) chocolates, both domestic and imported. If you are preparing a chocolate dessert that contains very few other ingredients, such as a custard or a confection, the flavor and creaminess of an exotic chocolate can lend distinction, but in most recipes it makes no difference. In fact, it would be criminal to waste a fine chocolate in a cake where its subtleties are bound to be overshadowed by the addition of spices, sour cream, butter, or sugar.

Chocolate comes in several forms. The main difference among them lies in the sweetening. Unsweetened chocolate is bitter, very dark, and quite brittle. Taken out of hand, it is inedible, but in baking, it packs the biggest chocolate punch per pound.

Partially sweetened chocolates are also called bittersweet or semisweet, depending on the manufacturer. They vary in flavor and sweetness, but generally have about half the amount of chocolate solids as unsweetened chocolate, and four tenths of an ounce of sugar is added to every ounce of chocolate.

Fully sweetened chocolates are called sweet chocolate if they are dark in color, milk chocolate if they are light. Both types have more sugar and less chocolate solids. Milk chocolate has an addition of dry milk solids.

This means that sweetened chocolates are not only sweeter than unsweetened products but are less chocolaty, too. That's why it is quite tricky to substitute one type of chocolate for another in a recipe. The difference will not just be a question of sweetness; rather, the entire flavor will change. So when substituting a sweetened chocolate for an unsweetened one, add about 1 teaspoon of cocoa powder for each ounce of chocolate. If substituting unsweetened chocolate for semisweet, cut the amount of chocolate by half and increase the amount of sugar by 25 percent.

Cocoa powder is unsweetened chocolate that has about 75 percent of its fat removed. In a cake, it produces a darker and more chocolate-tasting product. European cocoas are Dutch-processed, which means the chocolate is treated with a mild alkaline, causing the cocoa to become milder, darker, and more easily mixed in liquid. Although I prefer Dutched cocoa for making hot chocolate, I find that its taste is flat in baking unless in a batter with more acidic ingredients, such as the Chocolate Linzer Torte (page 52) with its layer of sweet-tart raspberry preserves.

White chocolate is not chocolate at all. Pardon my bluntness, but what we buy as white chocolate is really nothing more than sweet vanilla-flavored fat. However, because it is an emulsion, like chocolate, white chocolate has the same sensitivities to moisture and heat—and should be handled with the same precautions.

About Other Ingredients

Buttermilk. The acidic nature of buttermilk is essential to the texture of many desserts. If you don't have any on hand and would rather not buy an entire quart, substitute the same quantity of a fifty-fifty mixture of either plain yogurt and milk or sour cream and milk.

Coffee. When a dessert calls for instant-coffee powder, use any brand. Freeze-dried coffee is fine.

Dried citrus peel. Minced dried lemon and orange peels are sold in the spice section of many supermarkets. Using them will save you labor and cleanup, but freshly grated or minced citrus zest can be substituted for the dried product without adjusting measurement.

Dried fruit. Several of the recipes call for dried fruits, including raisins (both golden and dark), currants, cherries, and mixed diced fruit. The only ones you might not find at your supermarket are dried cherries; these are available in gourmet food stores and many health food stores and are well worth seeking out. Look for dried sour (or red) cherries for the best flavor.

One-Pot Chocolate Desserts

Eggs. The desserts were tested with both large and extra-large eggs; either size is fine.

Flour. All-purpose flour was used in testing; either bleached or unbleached is fine.

Milk. Use any kind of milk you have on hand. Fat content will not affect these recipes.

Nuts. The nuts specified in these recipes are varieties that are available already ground, so you can avoid using another piece of kitchen equipment if that's your preference. In fact, many other nut varieties work perfectly well in these recipes. If you don't mind the extra time and cleanup of grinding them yourself, go ahead and use them.

Sour cream. Either regular or reduced-fat sour cream can be used, but nonfat sour cream will not work in baking.

Vegetable oil sprays. These sprays make greasing a cake pan a two-second task.

Yogurt. These recipes were tested with low-fat yogurt, but any yogurt will work.

About the Techniques

Grinding nuts. Preground nuts help minimize cleanup, but if you have a food processor and an extra minute or two, grinding nuts yourself is a snap. Measure about 25 percent more nut pieces than the volume of ground nuts that the recipe calls for (if using a weight measure, the measurement stays the same). Pulse the nuts in two or three bursts of no more than 5 seconds' duration to coarsely chop them. Continue pulsing in shorter bursts until the nuts are uniformly ground into a powder as fine as sand. The object is to grind the nuts as fine as possible without transforming them into nut butter. So if they begin to clump or look oily, stop the processor and use them as they are.

Mashing bananas. When a batter calls for bananas, the fruit should be very ripe to allow them to be easily mashed with the back of a serving fork or wooden spoon and to ensure a better-tasting cake. Don't worry about leaving a few small lumps. Like chocolate chips and raisins, a few banana chunks will add flavor and texture.

Melting butter and chocolate. In recipes that specify melting butter and/or chocolate, use a heavy-bottomed, 3-quart saucepan for mixing the batter. Begin melting the butter over a flame, but then take it off the flame and let the residual heat finish the job of melting. When a recipe asks for melted chocolate, break the chocolate into pieces by hand and add the pieces after the butter has melted about halfway. The melted butter protects the chocolate from scorching, so you may keep the chocolate over the flame until it is about half melted. Then allow the residual heat to finish the melting.

Pinching baking powder and soda. To avoid any lumping, measure baking powder and soda into your hand, then pinch them in with your fingers to break up any lumps before adding them to a batter. Add baking soda and powder to the batter before the flour. Stir well, but if a few streaks appear don't be concerned. These will disappear when you stir in the flour.

About the Baking Pans

In recipes that call for melting butter and/or chocolate, use a heavy-bottomed, 3-quart saucepan for mixing the batter. It doesn't matter what type of metal the saucepan is made of. In recipes that don't require melting ingredients, use that same saucepan or a large mixing bowl. Although the types of desserts included in these pages vary widely, I've limited baking pans to those found in a typical home kitchen:

- 8- and 9-inch layer pans
- 9-inch square baking pan
- 2- and 3-quart casseroles (soufflé dishes)
- 9-inch cheesecake pan
- 9 × 5 × 3-inch loaf pan
- 9-inch springform
- 10-inch tube pan
- 10-inch Bundt pan
- 9 × 13 × 2-inch baking pan
- 10 × 15 × 1-inch jellyroll pan
- 12-cup standard muffin tin

One of the most talked about variables in baking is the color of the pan. I don't consider this as crucial as you may have been led to believe it is, but glass and dark-colored metal

One-Pot Chocolate Desserts

absorb heat faster than shiny metal pans. Far more important are your oven's temperature and the likelihood that it has some hot and cold spots. If you've noticed that some of your baking pans transfer heat faster than others, lower the oven heat by 25 degrees when using those pans.

Greasing the pan with vegetable oil spray or softened butter can help prevent cakes from sticking to the pan. Adding flour to a greased pan helps, too. After greasing, toss a small amount of flour into the pan and shake and rotate the pan until lightly coated with flour. Toss out any excess flour.

Cakes that have a tendency to stick, like tortes and brownies, benefit from lining the pan with kitchen parchment paper or foil. Trim a sheet of parchment or foil to the size of a round cake pan by setting the pan on the paper and tracing a circle. Cut inside the line and trim a little more if necessary to fit the paper inside the pan.

To remove a cake from the pan, allow it to cool in the pan for about 10 minutes. In that time, the cake will become a little sturdier and will release from the pan without cracking. Run a small, sharp knife around the edge of the cake to loosen it. Then cover the cake with wax paper, top with a rack or a large flat plate, and invert. The cake will fall from the pan. Remove the pan, cover with a cooling rack, and invert again. Remove the top rack or plate and paper, and cool for about 15 more minutes.

Very soft cakes, such as cheesecakes, need extra help. Don't use a knife. Rather, loosen the edge by holding the warm pan on its side and let gravity pull the cake down. Rotate the pan a quarter turn and let the cake drop again. Keep turning until the cake has been released all around.

If the cake won't come out of the pan, shake the inverted pan vigorously from side to side. If the cake still won't come out, sharply rap the pan and its covering plate on the countertop to break any sticky spots across the bottom of the cake. If this doesn't work, turn the cake right side up and loosen the edge again with a knife, but this time push the edge of the cake away from the side of the pan with the blade of the knife. Invert again. If it still won't come out, slice the cake right in the pan and lift the pieces out with a flexible spatula.

About Water Baths

Baked custards and puddings are apt to overbake along their edges before their centers are fully set. To protect the edges and slow down the heat transference, some of these desserts are baked in a larger pan of water. To prepare a water bath, place the unbaked pudding in a wider pan that is at least 2 inches deep but not deeper than the pudding pan. Place in the preheated oven and, using a pitcher, fill the larger pan with water. Remove the finished custard, flan, or pudding from the water bath as soon as it tests done.

One-Pot Chocolate Desserts

Chocolate Cakes

What is the perfect chocolate cake? Moist and brownie-dense, or angel-light and stained with cocoa? Is it plain and austere, delighting in nothing but its own chocolateness, or is it a six-layer ostentation, stacked with mousse and lacquered with hot fudge?

My own vision is pure American and decidedly preadolescent. The cake is buttery soft, moist enough to clog the tines of a fork, and always accompanied by an unlimited supply of cold milk. Ideally, it is eaten in solitude while watching cartoons, but I wouldn't object to the company of a good friend, or my little sister, provided that I don't have to share.

When I was cooking my way through *One-Pot Cakes,* I tried lots of chocolate cakes. And though all of them were very good, and some became new favorites, none fulfilled my nostalgic view of what a chocolate cake could be. They were either too rich, or too moist, or so loaded with nuts or infused with booze as to make them too grown-up.

But this time I've re-created my childhood dream cake. Twice, in fact. And I'm grateful for the second chance.

The Chocolate Buttermilk Layer Cake and the Brown Sugar Chocolate Cake that follow are frosted and unfrosted versions of my first passions. Though the buttermilk cake is a bit softer and the brown sugar cake a little smoother, they are both classics of the genre.

Brown Sugar Chocolate Cake

The roasted character of the molasses flavor of the brown sugar and coffee reinforces the choco-
late, so this cake uses less chocolate to greater effect. As I've said before, this is the cake I was
striving for in One-Pot Cakes. *It has a delicate, velvet crumb that stays moist for days without*
ever seeming wet.

Makes 12 servings

^{1}/2 pound (2 sticks) unsalted butter

3 ounces unsweetened chocolate, broken in
   large pieces

1^1/2 cups firmly packed dark brown sugar

1 teaspoon vanilla extract

3 eggs

1 teaspoon baking soda

2^1/4 cups flour

1 cup water or leftover cold coffee

Preheat the oven to 350°F. Grease a 10-inch Bundt pan or tube pan. Set aside.

In a large, heavy-bottomed saucepan over medium heat, begin melting the butter. When
it is half melted, add the chocolate, remove from the heat when the chocolate is half melted,
and stir until the butter and chocolate are completely melted. Mix in the brown sugar, vanilla, and eggs.

Add the baking soda in pinches and stir well. Stir in the flour and beat until it is well incorporated and the batter is thick. Stir in the water or coffee.

Pour and scrape the batter into the prepared pan and bake for 35 minutes, or until a
tester inserted into the crack of the cake comes out clean.

Cool on a rack for 10 minutes. Cover with a rack and invert. Remove pan. Allow cake to
cool to room temperature.

If desired, drizzle with Brown Butter Bourbon Chocolate Glaze (page 74).

Chocolate Carrot Cake

This cake was born by accident. About 20 minutes after I slid the completed layers into the oven, I realized I had forgotten to add the oil. At that point, there was nothing to do but finish baking and try again. But when I checked on the cake, it looked fine. And when I tasted it, I was floored. The cake was delicious—moist, tender, with the perfect blend of chocolate and spice. After a day, the oil-less cake began to toughen. But replacing some of the oil fixed that. The finished recipe calls for less than half the oil of a traditional carrot cake.

Makes 12 servings

4 eggs

1 1/2 cups sugar

1/4 cup cocoa powder

1/3 cup vegetable oil

2 teaspoons vanilla extract

2 teaspoons ground cinnamon

1/4 teaspoon salt

2 teaspoons baking soda

2 cups flour

5 cups grated carrots or 1 pound carrots, peeled and grated

1 cup white chocolate chips

1 cup pecan pieces

1 cup raisins

Preheat the oven to 350°F. Grease and flour two 8-inch layer cake pans. Set aside.

In a large bowl, mix the eggs until well blended. Mix in the sugar and cocoa until thoroughly combined. Mix in the oil, vanilla, cinnamon, and salt. Add the baking soda in pinches, breaking up any lumps with your fingers. Stir in thoroughly. Stir in the flour and beat until smooth. Mix in the grated carrots, white chocolate chips, pecans, and raisins just until they are evenly distributed.

Pour and scrape the batter into the prepared pans and bake for 40 to 45 minutes, or until a tester inserted in the center comes out clean.

Cool in the pans on a rack for 10 minutes. Unpan and cool completely. If desired, assemble the two layers into a single cake by frosting between the layers and around the sides, and top with a double recipe of Milk Chocolate Frosting (page 72).

Chocolate Buttermilk Layer Cake

This is a classic devil's food layer cake. Look for the quintessential birthday cake no further.

Makes 12 servings

¹/₄ cup water
1 tablespoon instant coffee powder
1 cup semisweet chocolate chips
¹/₄ pound (1 stick) unsalted butter
¹/₄ teaspoon salt
2 teaspoons vanilla extract
2 cups sugar
¹/₄ cup cocoa powder

3 eggs
1 cup buttermilk
1 teaspoon baking soda
2 cups plus 3 tablespoons all-purpose flour
Chocolate Sour Cream Icing (page 71), Milk Chocolate Frosting (page 72), or Deep Dark Chocolate Ganache (page 77)

Preheat oven to 350°F. Grease and flour two 9-inch layer pans. Set aside.

In a large, heavy saucepan, bring the water to a boil. Add the coffee powder, chocolate chips, and butter, and remove from the heat when the butter and chocolate have half melted. Stir until the butter and chocolate have completely melted.

Add the salt, vanilla, sugar, and cocoa, and mix until smooth. Stir in the eggs and the buttermilk. Add the baking soda in pinches, breaking up any lumps with your fingers, and stir until dissolved. Add the flour and mix until well blended.

Pour and scrape the batter into the prepared pans and bake for 30 minutes, or until a tester inserted in the center of the layers comes out with just a crumb clinging to it.

Cool on racks for 10 minutes. Cover each layer with a cooling rack, invert, and remove the pans. Cool right side up on racks.

To assemble, place one layer on a serving plate lined with its rim shielded by four strips of parchment or wax paper. Spread one third of the icing over the top of the layer. Top with the second layer. Spread one third of the icing over the sides of the cake and top with the remaining icing. Or stack the layers with the ganache, leaving the top without icing.

One-Pot Chocolate Desserts

Chocolate Orange Tea Cake

The acid from the orange juice acts as a tenderizer, just as buttermilk does in other cakes, in this fine-grained tea cake. The cake is also peppered with bits of candied orange peel. If possible, buy your orange peel from a fine confectionery. The mass-produced candied citrus sold in most super-markets is usually of inferior quality.

Makes 12 servings

1/2 **pound (2 sticks) unsalted butter**	**3 eggs**
3 ounces unsweetened chocolate, broken in large pieces	**1 teaspoon baking soda**
1 1/2 **cups firmly packed light brown sugar**	2 1/4 **cups flour**
1 teaspoon vanilla extract	1/4 **cup candied orange peel**
1/4 **teaspoon orange extract**	**1 cup orange juice**

Preheat the oven to 350°F. Grease a 10-inch Bundt pan or tube pan. Set aside.

In a large, heavy-bottomed saucepan over medium heat, begin melting the butter. When the butter is half melted, add the chocolate, remove from the heat when the chocolate is half melted, and stir until the butter and chocolate are completely melted. Mix in the brown sugar, vanilla and orange extracts, and eggs.

Add the baking soda in pinches, breaking up any lumps with your fingers, and stir well. Stir in the flour and beat until it is well incorporated and the batter is thick. Stir in the candied orange peel and the orange juice.

Pour and scrape the batter into the prepared pan and bake for 35 minutes, or until a tester inserted into the crack of the cake comes out clean.

Cool on a rack for 10 minutes. Cover with a rack and invert. Remove pan and let cool to room temperature.

If desired, drizzle with Brown Butter Bourbon Chocolate Glaze (page 74) or White Chocolate Nectar (page 69).

Chocolate Raspberry-Filled Cupcakes

In these cupcakes, a rich devil's food cake contains a rosy heart of raspberry jam. Just place the jam on top of the batter. As it bakes, the batter will rise and the jam will sink until it comes to rest in the very center of the cupcake. Be sure to use seedless raspberry preserves; seeds will ruin the cupcakes' texture.

Makes 12 servings

¹/4 **pound (1 stick) unsalted butter**
2 ounces unsweetened chocolate, broken in
   large pieces
1 cup firmly packed dark brown sugar
1 teaspoon instant coffee powder
1 teaspoon vanilla extract

2 eggs
1 teaspoon baking soda
1¹/2 cups flour
²/3 **cup water**
¹/4 **cup seedless raspberry preserves**

Preheat the oven to 350°F. Grease and flour the cups of a 12-cup muffin pan. Set aside.

In a large, heavy-bottomed saucepan over medium heat, begin melting the butter. When it is half melted, add the chocolate, remove from the heat when the chocolate is half melted, and stir until the butter and chocolate are completely melted. Mix in the brown sugar, coffee powder, and vanilla extract. Mix in the eggs.

Add the baking soda in pinches, breaking up any lumps with your fingers, and stir well. Stir in the flour and beat until it is well incorporated and the batter is thick. Stir in the water.

Spoon the batter into the prepared muffin pan, filling each cup about three-quarters full. Lay 1 teaspoon of raspberry preserves on the surface of each cup. The jam will sink down slightly. Bake for 15 minutes, or until each cupcake is firm.

Cool on a rack for 10 minutes. Lift each cupcake from the pan and let cool to room temperature.

Chocolate Chip Marble Coffee Cake

This recipe combines two of my favorite chocolate-infused cakes—chocolate chip tea cake and chocolate-swirled coffee cake. The chocolate chips are chilled in the freezer while the cake is prepared, which keeps them from melting when they are combined with the batter. You create a marbling effect by sprinkling cocoa, cinnamon, and sugar over the batter and stirring just enough to make streaks but not to blend them in.

Makes 12 servings

1 1/2 cups (12 ounces) mini-chocolate chips
12 tablespoons (1 1/2 sticks) unsalted butter
1 1/2 cups sugar
2 teaspoons vanilla extract
1/4 teaspoon salt
2 cups cold sour cream
2 eggs

1 1/2 teaspoons baking soda
1 1/2 teaspoons baking powder
3 cups flour
3 tablespoons packed dark brown sugar
3 tablespoons cocoa powder
1 tablespoon ground cinnamon

Place the chocolate chips in the freezer until ready to use. Preheat the oven to 350°F. Spray a heavy, nonstick 10-inch Bundt pan with spray shortening and set aside.

In a large, heavy saucepan over medium heat, begin melting the butter, stirring occasionally. When it is half melted, remove from the heat and stir until it is completely melted.

Stir in the sugar, vanilla, salt, sour cream, and eggs. Add the baking soda and baking powder in pinches, breaking up any lumps with your fingers. Stir thoroughly. Stir in the flour and beat until thoroughly blended. Stir in the chocolate chips.

Sprinkle the top of the batter with the brown sugar, cocoa, and cinnamon. Stir briefly— five strokes and no more.

Pour and scrape the batter into the prepared pan. Bake for 45 to 50 minutes, or until a tester inserted in the middle comes out with just a crumb clinging to it.

Cool on a rack for 5 minutes. Unpan and cool on the rack for at least 10 more minutes.

Chocolate Swirl Chocolate Chip Banana Cake

This banana cake, striated with chocolate and cinnamon, is extremely moist. It is a great cake to prepare ahead of time and keep on hand for several days. The bananas add an initial burst of moisture, and they continue delivering enough moisture to keep the cake from going stale for up to a week.

Makes 12 servings

1/2 pound (2 sticks) unsalted butter

2 cups sugar

6 very ripe bananas

1/2 cup sour cream (regular or reduced-fat but not fat-free)

2 teaspoons vanilla extract

Pinch salt

1 1/2 teaspoons baking soda

1 teaspoon baking powder

4 cups flour

3 ounces semisweet chocolate chips

3 tablespoons cocoa powder

1 tablespoon ground cinnamon

Preheat the oven to 350°F. Grease a 10-inch Bundt pan or tube pan. Set aside.

In a large, heavy saucepan, melt the butter over medium heat. Mix in the sugar and add the bananas, mashing them with the back of a fork or wooden spoon. Don't worry if the bananas remain lumpy.

Mix in the sour cream, vanilla, salt, baking soda, and baking powder. Stir in the flour and beat until all of it is well incorporated and the batter is thick. Stir in the chocolate chips.

Sprinkle the cocoa and cinnamon over the surface of the batter and swirl into the batter with no more than five strokes.

Pour and scrape the batter into the prepared pan and bake for 50 minutes, or until a tester inserted into the crack of the cake comes out clean. Cool on the rack for 10 minutes. Cover with a rack and invert. Remove pan. Cool right side up on rack.

One-Pot Chocolate Desserts

Chocolate Applesauce Spice Cake

Like all fruit or vegetable cakes, this one will stay fresh for up to a week. It is fragrant with spices and studded with bits of apple. If you want, serve it in a pool of warm Chocolate Honey (page 70).

Makes 9 to 12 servings

¹/₄ **pound (1 stick) unsalted butter**	**3 tablespoons cocoa powder**
1 cup sugar	**1 teaspoon vanilla extract**
1²/₃ **cups chunky applesauce**	**2 eggs**
¹/₈ **teaspoon ground allspice**	**2 teaspoons baking soda**
2 teaspoons ground cinnamon	**2 cups flour**
1 teaspoon ground ginger	**1 cup raisins**

Preheat the oven to 350°F. Grease and flour a 9-inch square baking pan. Set aside.

In a large saucepan over medium heat, melt the butter, stirring occasionally. Remove from the heat, and stir in the sugar, applesauce, allspice, cinnamon, ginger, cocoa powder, vanilla, and eggs. Add the baking soda in pinches, breaking up any lumps with your fingers. Stir thoroughly. Stir in the flour and beat until well blended. Stir in the raisins.

Pour the batter into the prepared pan and bake for 35 to 40 minutes, or until a tester inserted in the center comes out clean.

Cool in the pan on a rack for 10 minutes. Unpan and cool to room temperature.

Chocolate Pâté

As much confection as cake, this rich spicy loaf is chock-full of fruit, candy, and nuts bound together with a bare minimum of batter. The finished cake is a cross between chocolate fruitcake and dessert pâté. It needs no icing. Cut it in thin slices with a serrated knife.

Makes 16 servings

$^1/_2$ **cup milk**

$^1/_4$ **pound (1 stick) unsalted butter**

1 cup sugar

$^1/_2$ **teaspoon salt**

$^1/_4$ **cup cocoa powder**

1 teaspoon ground cinnamon

$^1/_2$ **teaspoon ground ginger**

2 eggs

1 teaspoon vanilla extract

2 teaspoons rum extract

1 teaspoon baking soda

2 cups flour

2 cups raisins

2 cups semisweet chocolate chips

2 cups walnut pieces

$^1/_3$ **cup chopped candied ginger (optional)**

Preheat oven to 350°F. Grease and flour a 9 × 5 × 3-inch loaf pan. Set aside.

In a heavy saucepan over medium heat, bring the milk to a simmer. Add the butter, and stir until the butter is melted. Remove from the heat and mix in the sugar, salt, cocoa, cinnamon, and ground ginger. Add the eggs and the vanilla and rum extracts, and mix until smooth.

Add the baking soda in pinches, breaking up any lumps with your fingers. Stir in thoroughly. Add the flour and mix until completely blended. Add the raisins, chocolate chips, walnut pieces, and candied ginger (if desired), and stir until the pieces are well distributed. Pour and scrape the batter into the prepared pan and bake for 1 hour and 15 minutes, or until a tester inserted in the center of the loaf comes out with just a crumb clinging to it. Cool in the pan on a rack for 15 minutes. Invert, remove pan, and cool upright on a rack to room temperature.

Cut with a serrated knife into thin slices.

One-Pot Chocolate Desserts

Black and White Almond Ring

This bicolored concoction with its shell of almond butter cake surrounding a center of chocolate devil's food seems to defy the one-pot notion. First, you assemble a white cake batter and pour half of it into a tube pan. You flavor the remaining batter with cocoa and pour it around the center of the ring. As the cake bakes, the white cake forms a shell around the chocolate, creating a graphic black and white design.

Makes 12 servings

¹/₂ **pound (2 sticks) unsalted butter**	**2 cups flour**
2 cups sugar	¹/₄ **cup finely ground almonds**
I teaspoon vanilla extract	¹/₂ **cup Amaretto**
I teaspoon almond extract	¹/₂ **cup milk**
3 eggs	**3 tablespoons cocoa powder**
I teaspoon baking powder	¹/₄ **teaspoon baking soda**

Preheat the oven to 350°F. Grease a 10-inch Bundt pan or tube pan. Set aside.

In a large, heavy saucepan, melt the butter over medium heat. Remove from the heat. Add the sugar, the vanilla and almond extracts, and the eggs. Beat until smooth.

Add the baking powder in pinches, breaking up any lumps with your fingers, and stir well. Stir in the flour and beat until the flour is well incorporated and the batter is thick. Stir in the almonds, Amaretto, and milk. Mix until the liquid has been completely incorporated. Pour and scrape half the batter into the prepared pan.

Mix the cocoa and baking soda into the remaining batter. Pour in a circle along the center of the ring of batter. Bake for 35 minutes, or until a tester inserted into the crack of the cake comes out clean.

Cool on a rack for 10 minutes. Cover with a rack and invert. Remove pan. Cool to room temperature.

Chocolate Brownies

The beauty of a brownie is in its contrast. The skin is dry and flaky atop a belly as pudgy as a puppy's, filled with moist fudge. The first bite yields without a fight, but each subsequent chew resists. Good brownies push back.

Because brownie batter has so little liquid, the moisture content of the finished product is controlled by underbaking. A perfectly baked batch of brownies should have a thin crust, a crackled and slightly risen edge, and a center that is still damp. A toothpick or skewer should emerge from the core with a bit of partially congealed batter clinging to it. This stickiness is the best sign that your steaming hot brownies will remain succulently moist once they have cooled.

Brownies are perfectly suited to the one-pot method. Their natural moistness and compacted texture are intensified by melting butter and chocolate together. And because most brownies require neither baking soda nor powder, sifting is never an issue.

One step might surprise you. When preparing the pan for baking brownies, I often line it with foil. This is a technique that is sometimes used with flourless cakes, which tend to break when you remove them from the pan. Brownies may not be flourless, but they are certainly flour-bereft. The foil will help hold the sheet of brownies together until they become firm enough to slice.

Triple-X Brownies

These brownies are the biggest, darkest, dampest, sweetest, over-the-top gargantuan examples of chocolate excess ever to pass between the lips of a chocoholic. The finished batter is quite moist and is a little tricky to cut, so it's best to make these brownies a day ahead. You will find that half a day in the refrigerator will make them much easier to cut into portions.

Makes 6 dozen small or 3 dozen large brownies

$^1/_2$ pound (2 sticks) unsalted butter	I tablespoon vanilla extract
8 ounces unsweetened chocolate, broken in pieces	5 eggs
$3^1/_2$ cups sugar	$1^3/_4$ cups flour
Pinch salt	2 cups whole almonds, skins on
	I cup semisweet chocolate chips

Preheat oven to 400°F. Line a 10 × 15 × 1-inch jellyroll pan with foil. Spray with spray shortening and set aside.

In a large, heavy-bottomed saucepan over medium heat, begin melting the butter. When it is half melted, add the chocolate, remove from the heat when the chocolate is half melted, and stir until the butter and chocolate are completely melted. Stir in the sugar, salt, vanilla, and eggs until mixture is smooth. Add the flour and stir until completely incorporated. Mix in the almonds and the chocolate chips.

Pour and scrape the batter into the prepared pan and bake for 30 minutes, or until the top is dry but the interior is still damp and has not yet firmed. Do not overbake.

Remove from the oven and cool in the pan on a rack for 10 minutes. Cover with a rack and invert. Remove pan and peel off foil. Replace pan and invert back into pan. Refrigerate until chilled through and solid.

Trim off edges and cut with a serrated knife into about 6 dozen small or 3 dozen large pieces. Store, unrefrigerated and wrapped in plastic, for up to 1 week, or freeze for up to several months.

Chocolate Chip Cookie Brownies

It is incredible that these impressive cookie-crusted bilevel brownies are made in a single vessel. A classic chocolate chip cookie dough is the base. Half of the dough becomes the crust while the remainder, with the addition of more eggs and some cocoa, is converted into a brownie batter.

Makes about 36 large pieces

$^3/_4$ **pound (3 sticks) unsalted butter**
2 cups packed light brown sugar
2 teaspoons vanilla extract
5 eggs
1 teaspoon baking soda

$3^1/_4$ **cups flour**
2 cups semisweet chocolate chips
$^1/_2$ **cup cocoa powder**
1 cup walnut pieces

Preheat oven to 400°F. Line a 10 × 15 × 1-inch jellyroll pan with foil. Spray with spray shortening and set aside.

In a large, heavy-bottomed saucepan over medium-high heat, melt the butter. Stir in the brown sugar, vanilla, and 3 of the eggs until smooth. Add the baking soda in pinches, mixing well. Mix in the flour and stir until the batter is completely smooth.

Pour and scrape half the batter into the prepared pan and spread in a thin, even layer. Sprinkle with the chocolate chips and press the chips into the batter.

Beat the remaining eggs and the cocoa into the batter until smooth. Mix in the walnuts. Pour and scrape into the prepared pan, over the layer of cookie dough, and spread evenly.

Bake on the lowest rack of the oven for 18 minutes, or until the top is dry but the interior is still damp and not yet firmed. Do not overbake.

Remove from the oven and cool in the pan on a rack for 10 minutes. Cover with a rack and invert. Remove pan and peel off foil. Replace pan and invert back into pan. Cool completely.

Trim edges and cut with a serrated knife into about 3 dozen large pieces. Store, unrefrigerated and wrapped in plastic, for up to 1 week, or freeze for up to several months.

One-Pot Chocolate Desserts

Toasty Walnut-Crusted Brownies

These brownies are nuts. The bottoms are crammed with sugar-glazed walnuts that toast right in the brownie pan, and the top is peppered with additional nuts that peek through the surface, burnishing to gold as the brownies bake.

Makes 25 brownies

2 ¹/₂ cups walnut pieces

2 tablespoons packed light brown sugar

¹/₂ pound (2 sticks) unsalted butter

6 ounces unsweetened chocolate, broken in pieces

1 teaspoon vanilla extract

2 ¹/₂ cups granulated sugar

5 eggs

2 cups flour

Preheat oven to 375°F. Line a 9-inch square cake pan with foil. Grease the foil.

Scatter half the walnuts in an even layer across the bottom of the pan, sprinkle the brown sugar on top of the nuts, and place in the preheated oven while you prepare the batter.

In a large, heavy-bottomed saucepan over medium heat, begin melting the butter. When it is half melted, add the chocolate, remove from the heat when the chocolate is half melted, and stir until the butter and chocolate are completely melted.

Add the vanilla, granulated sugar, eggs, and flour, and stir until the batter is smooth.

Remove the pan from the oven and place on a pot holder. Carefully pour and spoon the batter into the pan. Try to keep the walnuts in the pan in place. Smooth the top, then scatter the remaining walnuts over the top. Press down lightly.

Bake for 25 to 30 minutes, or until the cake is just set. Remove from the oven and cool on a rack for 10 minutes. Cover with a sheet pan and invert. Remove the baking pan. Loosen the foil, but do not remove it. Cover with a cooling rack and invert to finish cooling right side up.

Slice with a serrated knife into 25 brownies.

Chocolate Turtle Brownies

Loaded with heaping globs of chewy caramels and the crunch of roasted peanuts, Turtle Brownies are the cakey version of their namesake candy. Don't worry if the caramels begin to melt a bit into the batter. It helps them to blend and lends an intriguing nuance to the brownies.

Makes 25 brownies

$\frac{1}{2}$ pound (2 sticks) unsalted butter

6 ounces unsweetened chocolate, broken in pieces

1 teaspoon vanilla extract

24 soft caramel candies (about 7 ounces), such as Kraft

$2\frac{1}{2}$ cups sugar

5 eggs

2 cups flour

2 cups unsalted dry-roasted peanuts

Preheat oven to 350°F. Line a 10 × 15 × 1-inch jellyroll pan with foil. Grease the foil. Set aside.

In a large, heavy-bottomed saucepan over medium heat, begin melting the butter. When it is half melted, add the chocolate, remove from the heat when the chocolate is half melted, and stir until the butter and chocolate are completely melted.

Stir in the vanilla, caramels, sugar, eggs, and flour until the flour is fully blended. Stir in the peanuts.

Pour the batter into the prepared pan and smooth the top. The batter will nearly fill the pan.

Bake for 23 minutes, or until the cake is just set. Remove from the oven and cool on a rack for 10 minutes. Cover with a cooling rack and invert. Remove the pan and the foil. Cool upside down for 15 more minutes. Refrigerate until firm to aid in cutting.

Slice with a serrated knife into 25 brownies.

One-Pot Chocolate Desserts

Oatmeal Raisin Brownies

If you could cross-breed peanut butter crunch with oatmeal cookies and brownies, you would come up with this hearty, chewy, chunky brownie. The peanut butter is added to the hot butter, allowing it to melt gently. Don't try to save time by putting the peanut butter over direct heat; it will scorch before it liquefies.

Makes 25 brownies

$^1/_4$ **pound (1 stick) unsalted butter**
1 cup chunky peanut butter
2 teaspoons vanilla extract
1 cup packed dark brown sugar
1 cup granulated sugar
$^1/_4$ **cup cocoa powder**

4 extra-large eggs
1 cup raisins
1 cup semisweet chocolate chips
1 tablespoon baking soda
4 cups oatmeal (not instant)

Preheat oven to 350°F. Line a 10 × 15 × 1-inch jellyroll pan with foil. Grease the foil. Set aside.

In a large saucepan over medium heat, melt the butter. Add the peanut butter, and continue to stir until the peanut butter is half melted. Remove from the heat and stir until fully melted.

Stir in the vanilla, brown sugar, granulated sugar, cocoa powder, and eggs until the batter is smooth. Stir in the raisins and chocolate chips. Add the baking soda and beat vigorously to incorporate. Stir in the oats.

Pour the batter into the prepared pan and smooth the top. The batter will nearly fill the pan.

Bake for 23 minutes, or until the cake is just set. Remove from the oven and cool on a rack for 10 minutes. Cover with a cooling rack and invert. Remove the pan and the foil. Cool upside down for 15 more minutes. Invert onto another rack and cool completely.

Slice with a serrated knife into 25 brownies.

Very Chewy Brownies

The secret to making these brownies is replacing part of the flour with graham cracker crumbs. That simple alteration changes the flavor (the brownies develop a subtle nutty aroma), preserves the moisture content (the graham crackers soak up liquid and won't let it go), and makes the texture incredibly chewy.

Makes 25 brownies

$^1/_2$ pound (2 sticks) unsalted butter	1 tablespoon vanilla extract
$^1/_2$ pound unsweetened chocolate, broken in pieces	5 eggs
	$1^1/_3$ cups flour
$3^1/_2$ cups sugar	$1^1/_2$ cups graham cracker crumbs

Preheat oven to 375°F. Line a 10 × 15 × 1-inch jellyroll pan with foil. Grease the foil. Set aside.

In a large, heavy-bottomed saucepan over medium heat, begin melting the butter. When it is half melted, add the chocolate, remove from the heat when the chocolate is half melted, and stir until the butter and chocolate are completely melted.

Stir in the sugar, vanilla, and eggs until all are incorporated. Stir in the flour and beat well. Mix in the graham cracker crumbs.

Pour the batter into the prepared pan and smooth the top. The batter will nearly fill the pan.

Bake for 30 minutes, or until the cake is just set. Remove from the oven and cool on a rack for 10 minutes. Cover with a cooling rack and invert. Remove the pan and the foil. Cool upside down for 15 more minutes. Invert onto another rack and cool to room temperature.

Slice with a serrated knife into 25 brownies.

One-Pot Chocolate Desserts

Brownies à l'Orange

Fruit and chocolate form a symbiotic relationship. Each feeds off the other, increasing the power of both. Of all the fruit and chocolate combos, orange-chocolate is one of the most potent. Here, the orange power is doubled (from both dried orange peel and orange extract) and embellished with a bit of ginger.

Makes 25 brownies

12 tablespoons (1 1/2 sticks) unsalted butter	2 1/2 cups sugar
2 tablespoons dried orange peel	Pinch salt
1 teaspoon ground ginger	2 teaspoons orange extract
6 ounces unsweetened chocolate, broken in pieces	4 eggs
	1 1/4 cups flour

Preheat oven to 375°F. Line a 10 × 15 × 1-inch jellyroll pan with foil. Spray with spray shortening and set aside.

In a large, heavy-bottomed saucepan over medium-high heat, begin melting the butter. When it is half melted, add the orange peel and ginger, and continue cooking until the butter is completely melted. Add the chocolate. When the chocolate is half melted, remove the pan from the heat and stir until the chocolate is completely melted. Add the sugar, salt, orange extract, and eggs, and stir until smooth. Add the flour and beat until completely smooth.

Pour and scrape the batter into the prepared pan and bake for 20 to 25 minutes, or until the cake is just set. Remove from the oven and cool on a rack for 10 minutes. Cover with a cooling rack and invert. Remove the pan and the foil. Cool upside down for 15 more minutes. Invert onto another rack and cool to room temperature.

Slice with a serrated knife into 25 brownies.

White Chocolate Chocolate Chip Brownies

I have rarely had great success baking with white chocolate, except in tortes. So in this recipe, I took the formula for making a torte and turned it into brownies. The flour is replaced with ground nuts and cookie crumbs, and condensed milk is added, giving the brownies a cakey quality. The resulting brownies are very rich and inundated with walnuts.

Makes 24 brownies

12 tablespoons (1½ sticks) unsalted butter
4 ounces white chocolate, broken in pieces
2 cups graham cracker crumbs
½ cup ground walnuts

1 14-ounce can sweetened condensed milk
2 cups walnut pieces
12 ounces semisweet chocolate chips

Preheat oven to 350°F. Line a 9 × 13 × 2-inch baking pan with foil. Spray with spray shortening and set aside.

In a large, heavy-bottomed saucepan over medium-high heat, melt the butter. Add the white chocolate, reduce the heat to low, and stir until the chocolate is completely melted. Remove from heat. Stir in the graham cracker crumbs, ground walnuts, condensed milk, and walnut pieces. Stir in the chocolate chips.

Scrape the thick batter into the prepared pan. Moisten your hands with cold water and press the batter into an even layer. If the batter starts sticking to your hands, wet them again.

Bake for 25 minutes, or until lightly browned, crispy around the edge, and just set in the center. Remove from the oven and cool on a rack for 15 minutes. Cover with a cooling rack and invert. Remove the pan and the foil. Invert back into the pan and cool right side up to room temperature.

Slice with a serrated knife into 24 large brownies.

Black Forest Brownies

The combination of cherries and dark chocolate is a classic one, and deservedly so. Here, the cherries are scattered over the top of the raw batter, so they bake into and onto the finished brownies, creating a sticky chocolate-pocked glaze.

Makes 24 brownies

$^1/_2$ **pound (2 sticks) unsalted butter**	**I tablespoon vanilla extract**
$^1/_2$ **pound unsweetened chocolate, broken in pieces**	**5 eggs**
	$^3/_4$ **cup ground almonds**
$3^1/_2$ **cups sugar**	**I$^2/_3$ cups flour**

Preheat oven to 375°F. Spray the interior of a 9 × 13 × 2-inch baking pan with spray shortening. Set aside.

In a large, heavy-bottomed saucepan over medium heat, begin melting the butter. When it is half melted, add the chocolate, remove from the heat when the chocolate is half melted, and stir until the butter and chocolate are completely melted.

Stir in the sugar, vanilla, and eggs until smooth. Stir in the almonds and the flour and beat well.

Pour the batter into the prepared pan and smooth the top. Spoon the pie filling as evenly as possible over the surface of the batter. Spread gently with the back of your mixing spoon to make a solid layer. Don't worry if the cherries are not distributed perfectly.

Bake for 45 minutes, or until the cake is just set. Remove from the oven and cool on a rack to room temperature. Slice into 24 brownies and remove with a flexible spatula.

Spiced Brownie Brittle

These paper-thin cookie-cakes redefine what a brownie can be. Not too sweet, intensely choco-laty, and redolent with spice, they are a decidedly adult treat, the perfect companion for a cup of espresso. Notice that you do not grease the pan for these brownies. The proportion of butter to flour is so delicately balanced that added fat on the pan can cause the batter to split. Besides, these cookies never stick.

Makes 24 servings

1/4 pound (1 stick) unsalted butter
1 ounce unsweetened chocolate, broken in
   half
1/2 teaspoon ground ginger
1/2 teaspoon ground cinnamon
1/4 teaspoon ground black pepper

1/2 cup sugar
1/4 teaspoon vanilla extract
1 egg
1/3 cup flour
1/2 cup ground pecans, almonds, or walnuts

Preheat oven to 375°F.

In a large saucepan over medium heat, melt the butter. Add the chocolate, ginger, cinnamon, and black pepper. Remove from the heat and stir until the chocolate is melted.

Stir in the sugar, vanilla, and egg until smooth. Stir in the flour and beat well.

Pour and scrape the batter into a 10 × 15 × 1-inch jellyroll pan and tilt the pan back and forth, allowing the batter to flow into a thin, even layer across the pan. Scatter the ground nuts evenly over the top.

Bake for 10 minutes, or until the cake is just set. Remove from the oven and cool on a rack for 20 minutes. Cut or break into 2 dozen rough-shaped pieces, as you would a nut brittle.

One-Pot Chocolate Desserts

Chocolate Puddings, Custards, and Cheesecakes

No Proustian madeleine for me. It's chocolate pudding that makes me quiver. Just a spoonful is enough to reawaken childhood memories of its milky perfume perking in a pot, the comfort in every spoonful that shimmied down my throat.

Pudding-eating tends to fade with age, its innocent charms eclipsed by an acquired decadent taste for pôts de crème and chocolate mousse. Yet the joy of pudding does not need to be reserved for childhood. Not only is its appeal universal, but its form can be universally varied.

Custard, flan, cheesecake, bread pudding, rice pudding, and kugel share a common heritage. They are all sweetened dairy products bound with egg and heated until set. The form of dairy used—milk, cream, or cheese—differentiates a custard from a pôt de crème from a cheesecake. The sugar can be caramelized or not. The egg can stand alone, it can be fortified with yolks, or it can be partially replaced with cornstarch.

Beyond these changes in ingredients, the proof of many a pudding is in how it's cooked. Creamy puddings are simmered in a saucepan. Formed puddings are baked or steamed in a mold, sometimes with bread cubes, cooked rice, or noodles, to help them set.

Regardless of how a pudding is cooked, it is always handled with care. Puddings can't be rushed or cooked at high temperatures. They set at a specific point, and only a split second stands between velvety thickness and a pot full of curds.

It is this need for caution that has led to my strange way of baking cheesecakes. I slow the process down. And when I say slow, I mean *slow*. I set the oven at 200°F and bake the cake for 8 hours. I know this sounds nuts, but the timing fits so well with my sleeping schedule that I would never bake a cheesecake any other way. I mix up the batter right before retiring, place it in the oven, go off to bed, and, voilà, in the morning I'm greeted by a finished dessert. Because the oven temperature is so low, minimal energy is used, and because of the unique chemistry of custards, the reduced temperature and increased cooking time coax the ingredients into a semisolid consistency that is the quintessence of cheesecake.

If you are in a rush, or if you're just plain nervous about leaving your oven on for so long, any of the cheesecakes in this chapter can be baked at 350°F for 1 1/2 hours. But the results will not be nearly as creamy or pristine. If you do bake them at a higher temperature, you will need to place the cake in a pan of water while it bakes to keep the temperature of the baking pan from rising past 212°F (the temperature of boiling water). With the slower method, the oven temperature is so low that a water bath is unnecessary.

One word of warning: All cream cheeses are not created equal. It is perfectly fine to use regular or reduced-fat cream cheese, but don't attempt these recipes with fat-free products. And don't try them with budget brands, either. These are loaded with vegetable gums, which will keep the cream cheese from blending smoothly. The brand of cream cheese I use with consistently good results is Philadelphia, made by Kraft. All cheesecakes will keep for a week under refrigeration and can be frozen for up to 1 month.

One-Pot Chocolate Desserts

Very Chocolate Cheesecake

The notion of chocolate cheesecake has always seemed redundant to me. Each of the two major ingredients seems too in-and-of-itself ever to want or need companionship from the other. But sure enough, when combined they explode in over-the-top overindulgence.

Makes 16 to 20 servings

1/2 cup cocoa powder	2 pounds cream cheese, regular or reduced-
3/4 cup milk	fat, at room temperature
2 tablespoons instant coffee powder	2 teaspoons vanilla extract
4 ounces unsweetened chocolate, broken in	3 tablespoons cognac
pieces	5 eggs
2 cups sugar	

Preheat the oven to 200°F. Thoroughly grease the inside of a 3-quart soufflé dish with spray shortening and dust with 1/4 cup of the cocoa powder. Tap out any excess. Set aside.

In a large, heavy saucepan, combine the milk, remaining cocoa, and coffee powder, and bring to a boil. Add the chocolate, let the chocolate partially melt, then remove from the heat and stir with a wooden spoon until the chocolate has completely melted and the coffee and cocoa are completely dissolved.

Stir in the sugar until blended. Add the cream cheese and mix until completely smooth. Mix in the vanilla, cognac, and eggs just until blended. Do not overmix.

Pour and scrape the batter into the prepared soufflé dish and bake for 6 to 8 hours or overnight. Cool on a rack to room temperature. Cover with a sheet of plastic wrap or wax paper and an inverted plate. Invert, remove the cake from the pan, and refrigerate upside down for at least 1 hour. (If you need to leave the house, the cake can stay refrigerated all day.) Invert a serving plate over the cheesecake and invert the cake. Remove the top plate and the paper. Cover and refrigerate.

Cut with a long, sharp knife dipped in warm water to prevent sticking.

Chocolate Orange Chocolate Chip Cheesecake

If you think chocolate cheesecake is rich, this version will send you into cardiac-arresting ecstasy. The chocolate–cream cheese batter is laced with orange liqueur and punctuated with chocolate chips.

Makes 16 to 20 servings

1 cup cocoa powder, preferably
   Dutch-processed
2 pounds cream cheese (regular or
   reduced-fat), at room temperature
1 1/2 cups sugar

2 tablespoons vanilla extract
2 teaspoons orange extract
1/4 cup orange liqueur
5 eggs
12 ounces mini-chocolate chips

Preheat oven to 200°F. Spray the interior of a 2-quart soufflé dish or 9-inch cheesecake pan with spray shortening and dust with 1/4 cup of the cocoa. Set aside.

In a large bowl, mix the cream cheese and the sugar until smooth and soft, scraping the sides of the bowl and spoon, as necessary. Mix in the remaining 3/4 cup of cocoa, vanilla and orange extracts, liqueur, and eggs until the batter is well blended. Stir in the chocolate chips.

Pour and scrape the batter into the prepared pan and place in the oven. Bake for 6 to 8 hours or overnight. Cool on a rack to room temperature. Cover with a sheet of plastic wrap or wax paper and an inverted plate. Invert. Remove the pan and refrigerate cake upside down for at least 1 hour. (If you need to leave the house, the cake can stay refrigerated all day.) Invert a serving plate over the cheesecake and invert the cake. Remove the top plate and the paper. Cover and refrigerate until ready to serve.

Cut with a long, sharp knife dipped in warm water to prevent sticking.

Chocolate Cannoli Cheesecake

This rendition of an Italian cheesecake takes its inspiration from the filling in a chocolate cannoli. The chocolate ricotta custard is strewn with raisins, chocolate bits, and walnuts, and laced with rum.

Makes 16 to 20 servings

1 cup cocoa powder, preferably Dutch-processed
1/2 cup water
1 cup raisins
1 pound cream cheese (regular or reduced-fat), at room temperature
1 pound ricotta cheese (whole or part-skim), drained
2 tablespoons sour cream (regular or reduced-fat, but not fat-free)

1 1/2 cups sugar
1 tablespoon vanilla extract
1/4 cup dark rum
5 eggs
24 chocolate wafers, broken into small pieces
1 cup walnut pieces

Preheat oven to 200°F. Spray the interior of a 2-quart soufflé dish or 9-inch cheesecake pan with spray shortening, dust with 1/4 cup of the cocoa, and set aside.

In a large saucepan, bring the water to a boil. Add the raisins and boil until the water is reduced by half and the raisins are plump. Remove from the heat.

Stir in the remaining 3/4 cup cocoa, the cream cheese, ricotta cheese, sour cream, and sugar, and beat with a wooden spoon until the mixture is smooth and soft. Mix in the vanilla, rum, and eggs until well blended. Fold the chocolate wafers and the walnut pieces into the batter.

Pour and scrape the batter into the prepared soufflé dish and bake for 6 to 8 hours or overnight. Cool on a rack to room temperature. Cover with a sheet of plastic wrap or wax paper and an inverted plate. Invert. Remove the pan and refrigerate the cake upside down for at least 1 hour. Invert a serving plate over the cheesecake and invert the cake. Remove the top plate and the paper. Cover and refrigerate until ready to serve.

Cut with a long, sharp knife dipped in warm water to prevent sticking.

Cherry Chocolate Swamp Cake

This cake—dense, fudgy, and resting on a swamp of chocolate and cherries—has a homey presentation, and it is best served warm. The syrupy fruit becomes a natural sauce. If you make it ahead, be sure to let the cake rest in a low oven for about 15 minutes before serving.

Makes 12 to 16 servings

I cup flour
2 teaspoons baking powder
$^1/_2$ teaspoon baking soda
Pinch salt
$^1/_2$ cup sugar
6 tablespoons cocoa powder

$^1/_2$ cup milk
I teaspoon vanilla extract
$^1/_4$ cup vegetable oil
$^1/_2$ cup (firmly packed) dark brown sugar
I can or jar (21 or 24 ounces) cherry pie
   filling

Preheat the oven to 350°F. Grease a 9-inch square baking pan with spray shortening and set aside.

In a large mixing bowl, combine the flour, baking powder, baking soda, salt, sugar, and cocoa until thoroughly blended. Add the milk, vanilla, and oil, and stir until a thick batter forms. Pour and scrape the batter into the prepared pan and spread into an even layer.

Sprinkle the brown sugar over the top in an even layer. Pour on the cherry pie filling and spread evenly.

Bake for 30 minutes, or until bubbly around the edges. Cool on a rack for 10 minutes.

Cut into squares and serve with a large spoon while still warm.

One-Pot Chocolate Desserts

Chocolate Rum Pudding Cake

Pudding cakes are the most casual of American desserts. Gooey and sweet, this one tastes excep-
tionally rich, even though it has just a bit more than 1 teaspoon of fat per serving. A thick batter
is spread over the bottom of a baking pan and topped with rum and hot water. While the cake
bakes, the batter rises as the liquid sinks to the bottom. Here, the finished product has a fudgy
layer of cake floating on a pool of rum-soaked chocolate sauce.

Makes 8 servings

1 cup flour	1/2 cup milk
2 teaspoons baking powder	1 teaspoon vanilla extract
1/2 teaspoon baking soda	1 teaspoon rum extract
1/4 teaspoon salt	1/4 cup vegetable oil
1 cup sugar	1/2 cup molasses
Pinch ground cinnamon	1/4 cup dark rum
1/2 cup cocoa powder	1/2 cup hot water

Preheat oven to 350°F.

Combine the flour, baking powder, baking soda, salt, 3/4 cup of the sugar, cinnamon, and half the cocoa. Add the milk, the vanilla and rum extracts, and oil, and mix into a thick batter.

Spread the batter evenly in a greased 9-inch square baking pan. Sprinkle the top with the remaining cocoa and sugar. Pour the molasses, rum, and hot water over all.

Bake for 30 minutes. The cake will be set around the sides, and the top will be very loose and bubbly. Cool in the pan on a rack for 10 minutes or more. Slice or scoop to serve.

Best-Ever Chocolate Pudding

The popularity of boxed puddings has left us with the mistaken notion that preparing pudding from scratch is beyond our abilities. But pudding always was, and still is, the easiest of all homemade desserts. This pudding is spectacular—densely chocolate and exceptionally creamy. You may never open a box of pudding mix again.

Makes 6 servings

$^3/_4$ cup sugar
Pinch salt
3 tablespoons cornstarch
3 tablespoons cocoa powder
3 cups milk

3 eggs
2 ounces semisweet chocolate, broken in
 pieces
2 teaspoons vanilla extract

In a large, heavy-bottomed saucepan, combine the sugar, salt, cornstarch, and cocoa. Add 1 cup of the milk and stir until the cornstarch is dissolved. Little bits of cocoa may still be visible, but they'll go away as the pudding cooks. Mix in the eggs. Add the remaining milk and stir to combine.

Place over medium heat and, stirring constantly, cook until the pudding thickens slightly and lumps appear on the bottom of your stirring spoon, about 5 minutes. Remove from heat and mix vigorously until the lumps blend in. Stir in the chocolate until melted.

Return pan to heat and cook pudding until boiling and thick, stirring constantly; be sure to stir thoroughly across the bottom of the pan and into the corners.

Remove pan from heat and stir in the vanilla. While still warm, pour pudding into six $^1/_2$-cup dessert dishes or bowls. Cover loosely with plastic wrap and chill.

If desired, serve garnished with whipped cream.

Chocolate Cheesecake Pudding

This pudding, which tastes like chocolate cheesecake in a bowl, is richer than the preceding chocolate pudding.

Makes 6 servings

³/₄ **cup sugar**
Pinch salt
3 tablespoons flour
¹/₄ **cup Dutch-processed cocoa**

3 cups milk
3 eggs
2 teaspoons vanilla extract
¹/₂ **pound cream cheese, softened**

In a large, heavy-bottomed saucepan, combine the sugar, salt, flour, and cocoa. Add 1 cup of the milk and stir until flour is incorporated. Little bits of cocoa may still be visible, but they'll go away as the pudding cooks. Beat in the eggs. Add the remaining 2 cups milk and stir to combine.

Place over medium heat and, stirring constantly, cook until the pudding comes to a boil and thickens slightly, and lumps appear on the bottom of your stirring spoon, about 5 minutes. Remove from heat and mix vigorously until the lumps blend in.

Return pan to heat and cook pudding until boiling and thick, stirring constantly; be sure to stir thoroughly across the bottom of the pan and into the corners.

Stir in the vanilla and cream cheese. While still warm, pour pudding into 6 dessert dishes or glasses. Cover loosely with plastic wrap and chill.

If desired, serve garnished with whipped cream.

Caramel Chocolate Flan

The caramel in this flan acts as both a sauce and a flavoring. Some of the caramelized sugar is poured into the baking dish; the rest is blended into the milk and transformed into this chocolate custard, with a dark chocolate upper layer, a caramel base, and a shimmering caramel sauce.

Makes 8 servings

1 1/2 cups sugar
4 cups milk
1/4 cup cocoa powder
Pinch salt

1/2 teaspoon ground cinnamon
2 teaspoons vanilla extract
5 eggs

Preheat oven to 350°F.

Heat the sugar in a heavy saucepan over medium-high heat. After 2 minutes, start stirring and continue to stir until the sugar melts into a pale golden caramel, about 2 more minutes. Pour about one third of the caramel into a 9-inch round baking dish. Carefully tilt the dish so the caramel evenly coats the bottom. Work quickly because the caramel will stop flowing if it cools. Set aside.

Add half the milk to the caramelized sugar remaining in the saucepan. It will bubble vigorously. Stir until the bubbling stops. Any caramel clinging to the pan will immediately solidify. Stir in the cocoa, salt, and cinnamon. Heat the milk to a simmer, stirring occasionally. Any solid pieces of caramel will melt into the milk. Remove from the heat.

Stir in the remaining 2 cups milk and the vanilla. Beat in the eggs until incorporated.

Pour into the caramel-lined baking dish and set dish in a larger pan of water. Bake for 1 hour, or until a knife inserted in the center comes out with just a speck of custard clinging to it. Let cool to room temperature on a rack and refrigerate for several hours until chilled.

To serve, run a knife around the perimeter of the custard and cover with a large rimmed tray. Invert the dish onto the tray. Shake lightly to release the custard. When the custard drops from the dish, lift off the dish, allowing the caramel sauce to run over the top of the flan and down onto the tray. Serve the flan in slices with a bit of sauce spooned on top.

One-Pot Chocolate Desserts

Chocolate Honey Pôt de Crème

Pôt de crème is the plushest of all custards. It should be baked in individual custard cups or ramekins. If you have neither, use small oven-safe dessert bowls, keeping in mind that since most dessert bowls are shallower than custard cups, the pôt de crème might cook faster. Just be sure to test it frequently to see that it doesn't overbake. Because pôt de crème is so rich, it will solidify as it cools, so its center should be quite loose when it is removed from the oven.

Makes 4 servings

2 cups (1 pint) light cream
4 ounces semisweet chocolate, broken in
  pieces
$^1/_4$ cup honey

$^1/_4$ teaspoon salt
$1^1/_2$ teaspoons vanilla extract
3 eggs

Preheat oven to 325°F.

Heat half the cream in a heavy saucepan over medium-high heat until bubbles form at the edge of the pan. Add the chocolate and stir until half melted. Remove from the heat and stir until the chocolate has completely melted.

Stir in the honey, remaining 1 cup cream, salt, and vanilla. Add the eggs and stir vigorously until completely incorporated.

Pour into 4 custard cups, ramekins, or ovenproof dessert dishes that have at least a $^3/_4$-cup capacity. Set the cups in a low-sided pan and pour 1 inch of water into the pan. Bake for 22 minutes. The custards should still be wet in their centers.

Remove from the pan and cool to room temperature, then refrigerate for at least 1 hour before serving.

If desired, the custards can be gilded with whipped cream and/or fresh berries.

Triple Chocolate Bread Pudding

Homey, wet, and dense, this chocolate bread pudding earns the "triple" in its name from using chocolate cake in place of bread, cocoa powder, and an avalanche of chocolate chips. You can bake this pudding ahead of time and serve it cold with White Chocolate Nectar (page 69) or Down and Dirty Hot Fudge Sauce (page 68) or serve it warm on its own right from the oven.

Makes 12 servings

4 cups milk

1 cup sugar

1/4 cup cocoa powder

2 teaspoons vanilla

4 eggs

1 chocolate loaf cake (15 or 16 ounces)

12 ounces semisweet chocolate chips

Preheat oven to 350°F.

In a heavy saucepan over medium heat, heat 2 cups of the milk, the sugar, and the cocoa until the sugar and cocoa dissolve, stirring often.

Remove from the heat and add the vanilla and the remaining 2 cups milk. Mix in the eggs until smooth. Crumble the cake into bite-sized pieces and stir into the custard. Stir in the chocolate chips. Pour into a 9 × 13 × 2-inch baking dish.

Bake for 1 hour until set almost all of the way into the middle. Remove from oven and cool on a wire rack for at least 15 minutes before serving. Serve warm or chilled.

Chocolate Tortes

One-pot cakes, by their very nature, are richer, smoother, more flavorful, and less aerated than cakes that incorporate air into the batter by beating. You cannot make an angel food or sponge cake with the one-pot method. But cakes that shun the ethereal in favor of something moist and decadent are improved by the one-pot process, among them fudge cakes, cheesecakes, and tortes. Especially tortes.

No one expects a torte to be light. In fact, the denser it is, the better. Such texture is guaranteed by a high proportion of chocolate, butter, and egg and the relative absence of flour.

In most torte recipes, flour is replaced by finely ground nuts. Although any type of nut will do, I've limited the nuts used in these recipes to those you can buy already ground—almonds, walnuts, pecans, and hazelnuts. To substitute macadamias for almonds, or black walnuts for pecans, grind them using a food processor (see page 5).

Tortes are less resilient than flour-based cakes and therefore have a greater chance of sticking to the pan and breaking when they are unmolded. To help prevent this, line the bottoms of their baking pans with parchment paper or foil. If a torte sticks, it will be to the paper rather than to the pan. When inverted, the torte will slip from the pan along with the paper, which can be easily peeled away.

Because they are so rich, tortes are always served as a single layer and in small slices. They can be presented with nothing more than a dusting of confectioners' sugar or, for more formal occasions, sheathed in a coating of chocolate glaze. Several recipes for glazes appear in the chapter starting on page 67, where you'll also find the technique for glazing a torte.

One-Pot Chocolate Desserts

Chocolate Mousse Torte

This pudding-cum-cake is as damp and dark as a torte can be. It's really a baked mousse—sinfully rich and needing no more than a few slices of fruit for garnish. If you want to go for broke, you can serve it topped with Chocolate Brandy Glaze (page 73).

Makes 16 servings

4 tablespoons (^{1}/2 stick) unsalted butter

5 ounces semisweet chocolate, broken in pieces

1 cup sugar

2 tablespoons cocoa powder

^{1}/4 teaspoon salt

1 teaspoon vanilla extract

3 eggs

1 teaspoon baking powder

^{1}/4 cup all-purpose flour

Preheat oven to 325°F. Coat the interior of a 9-inch springform pan with spray shortening. Line the bottom with parchment paper or foil (see page 7). Spray the paper. Set aside.

In a large, heavy-bottomed saucepan over medium heat, begin melting the butter. When it's half melted, add the chocolate, remove the pan from the heat when the chocolate is half melted, and stir until the butter and chocolate are completely melted.

Add the sugar, cocoa, salt, and vanilla, and stir until smooth. Beat in the eggs until completely incorporated. Add the baking powder in pinches to break up any lumps and stir to incorporate. Stir in the flour.

Pour and scrape the batter into the prepared pan and bake for 40 minutes, or until the top is dry but a tester inserted in the center comes out with a damp crumb clinging to it. Do not overbake.

Remove from the oven and cool in the pan on a rack for 30 minutes. Run a knife around the edge of the cake, remove the sides of the springform, and cool for another 30 minutes. Cover with a rack and invert. Remove pan bottom and paper. Turn upright and continue to cool until cake is at room temperature.

Serve in thin slices, garnished with whipped cream and fresh berries, if desired.

Mocha Walnut Torte

This delicious torte is lighter in both color and flavor than other chocolate tortes. Walnut is the flavor that predominates. Serve the torte with Chocolate Honey (page 70) or Deep Dark Chocolate Ganache (page 77).

Makes 10 servings

¹/₄ cup water (see Note)

2 tablespoons instant coffee powder (see Note)

¹/₄ pound (1 stick) unsalted butter

2 ounces semisweet chocolate, broken in pieces

²/₃ cup packed light brown sugar

3 eggs

1³/₄ cups ground walnuts

1 teaspoon vanilla extract

Confectioners' sugar (optional)

Preheat oven to 375°F. Grease an 8- or 9-inch layer pan. Line the bottom with parchment paper or foil (see page 7). Grease the paper and set aside.

In a large, heavy saucepan over high heat, bring the water to a boil. Add the coffee and stir to dissolve. Add the butter and melt. Add the chocolate, and when it has begun to melt, remove from the heat and stir until it is completely melted. Mix in the brown sugar. Mix in the eggs, walnuts, and vanilla.

Pour and scrape the batter into the prepared pan and bake for 25 minutes, or until a tester inserted in the center comes out with only a moist crumb clinging to it. Do not overbake. Cool in the pan on a rack for 20 minutes. Remove from pan, peel off paper, and let cool to room temperature. Dust with confectioners' sugar, if desired.

Note: In place of the water and instant coffee, you can use ¹/₂ cup brewed coffee. Just bring to a boil and boil vigorously until reduced by half, about 2 minutes.

Chocolate Coconut Torte

Whether your family traditions center on chocolate Easter eggs, chocolate-glazed macaroons, or chocolate coconut patties, the magic combination of cocoa and coconut is instantly nostalgic. The flavor has been modernized with the subtle scents of almond and orange.

Makes 10 servings

$1/4$ **pound (1 stick) unsalted butter**	**3 eggs**
4 ounces semisweet chocolate, broken in pieces	**2 tablespoons dried orange peel**
	1 teaspoon vanilla extract
$2/3$ **cup sugar**	$1/4$ **teaspoon almond extract**
$1 2/3$ **cups shredded unsweetened coconut**	**Chocolate Brandy Glaze (page 73)**

Preheat oven to 375°F. Grease an 8- or 9-inch layer pan, line the bottom with parchment paper or foil (see page 7), grease the paper, and set aside.

In a large, heavy-bottomed saucepan over medium heat, begin melting the butter. When it is half melted, add the chocolate, remove pan from the heat when the chocolate is half melted, and stir until the butter and chocolate are completely melted. Mix in the sugar. Mix in the coconut, eggs, orange peel, and vanilla and almond extracts.

Pour and scrape the batter into the prepared pan and bake for 25 minutes, or until a tester inserted in the center comes out with only a moist crumb clinging to it. Do not over-bake. Cool in the pan on a rack for 20 minutes, remove from pan, and peel off paper. Let cool to room temperature.

Prepare and ice with Chocolate Brandy Glaze.

Chocolate Cognac Torte

Dried currants simmered in cognac give this torte the fruity flavor of aged brandy. It is particularly luscious topped with Brown Butter Bourbon Chocolate Glaze (page 74).

Makes 10 servings

¹/₂ cup dried currants

3 tablespoons cognac

¹/₄ pound (1 stick) unsalted butter

4 ounces semisweet chocolate, broken in pieces

²/₃ cup sugar

3 eggs

1 cup plus 2 tablespoons (5¹/₃ ounces) ground almonds

1 teaspoon vanilla extract

Confectioners' sugar

Preheat the oven to 375°F. Grease an 8- or 9-inch layer pan, line the bottom with parchment paper or foil (see page 7), grease the paper, and set aside.

In a large, heavy saucepan over low heat, cook the currants in the cognac until all the liquid has been absorbed, about 2 minutes. Add the butter. When it is half melted, add the chocolate, remove the pan from the heat when the chocolate is half melted, and stir until the butter and chocolate are completely melted. Remove from the heat and mix in the sugar. Mix in the eggs, almonds, and vanilla.

Pour and scrape the batter into the prepared pan and bake for 25 minutes, or until a tester inserted in the center comes out with only a moist crumb clinging to it. Do not overbake. Cool in the pan on a rack for 20 minutes, remove from pan, and peel off paper. Let cool to room temperature.

Serve dusted with confectioners' sugar.

One-Pot Chocolate Desserts

Chocolate Ginger Torte

The tang of this torte comes from ginger preserves, which give all the spicy sweetness of candied ginger without your having to do any chopping. Ginger preserves, generally sold along with jellies and jams, should not be confused with preserved ginger, an Asian product usually served with sushi. Ginger preserves are mostly imported, and if available at your local supermarket, might be found in the gourmet section.

Makes 10 servings

$^1/_4$ **pound (1 stick) unsalted butter**
1 teaspoon ground ginger
4 ounces semisweet chocolate, broken in pieces
$^2/_3$ **cup sugar**
$^1/_3$ **cup ginger preserves**

3 eggs
$1^2/_3$ **cups (8 ounces) ground almonds**
$^1/_2$ **teaspoon vanilla extract**
$^1/_4$ **teaspoon almond extract**
Confectioners' sugar

Preheat oven to 375°F. Grease an 8- or 9-inch layer pan, line the bottom with parchment paper or foil (see page 7), grease the paper, and set aside.

In a large, heavy saucepan over low heat, melt the butter with the ground ginger. Add the chocolate, remove the pan from the heat when the chocolate is half melted, and stir until the butter and chocolate have completely melted. Remove from the heat and mix in the sugar. Mix in the ginger preserves, eggs, almonds, and vanilla and almond extracts.

Pour and scrape the batter into the prepared pan and bake for 25 minutes, or until a tester inserted in the center comes out with only a moist crumb clinging to it. Do not over-bake. Cool in the pan on a rack for 20 minutes. Remove from pan and peel off paper or foil. Cool to room temperature.

Serve dusted with confectioners' sugar.

White Chocolate Praline Torte

This buttery white chocolate torte combines the bitter nuance of pecans, the scent of orange zest, and a hint of brandy. It can be elegantly cloaked with Brown Butter Bourbon Chocolate Glaze (page 74) and accompanied by sections of clementine or tangerine.

Makes 10 servings

6 tablespoons unsalted butter

6 ounces white chocolate chips

$^{1}/_{2}$ cup honey

1 tablespoon dried orange peel

2 tablespoons brandy

3 eggs

$1^{2}/_{3}$ cups ground pecans

Preheat oven to 375°F. Grease an 8- or 9-inch layer pan, line the bottom with parchment paper or foil (see page 7), grease the paper, and set aside.

In a large, heavy saucepan over medium heat, begin melting the butter. When it's half melted, add the white chocolate and stir briefly. Remove from the heat and continue stirring until the butter and chocolate are completely melted. Mix in the honey, dried orange peel, brandy, and eggs until smooth. Mix in the pecans.

Pour and scrape the batter into the prepared pan and bake for 25 minutes, or until a tester inserted in the center comes out with only a moist crumb clinging to it. Do not over-bake. Cool in the pan on a rack for 20 minutes. Remove from pan and peel off paper or foil. Let cool to room temperature.

One-Pot Chocolate Desserts

Chocolate Toasted Hazelnut Torte

Although this torte can be made with any type of ground nut (almonds are especially good), hazelnuts are a natural with chocolate—if you take the time to toast them first. Here, the toasting is done by browning the nuts in the melted butter while the batter is being assembled.

Makes 10 servings

$^1/_4$ **pound (1 stick) unsalted butter**
$1^2/_3$ **cups ground hazelnuts**
**4 ounces semisweet chocolate, broken in
  pieces**
$^2/_3$ **cup sugar**

3 eggs
1 teaspoon vanilla extract
$^1/_4$ **teaspoon almond extract**
1 tablespoon brandy

Preheat oven to 375°F. Grease an 8- or 9-inch layer pan, line the bottom with parchment paper or foil (see page 7), grease the paper, and set aside.

In a large, heavy saucepan over medium-high heat, melt the butter. Add the hazelnuts and stir until the nuts are toasted, about 1 to 2 minutes. Add the chocolate, remove pan from heat, and continue stirring until chocolate is fully melted. Mix in the sugar. Mix in the eggs, the vanilla and almond extracts, and brandy.

Pour and scrape the batter into the prepared pan and bake for 25 minutes, or until a tester inserted in the center comes out with only a moist crumb clinging to it. Do not overbake. Cool in the pan on a rack for 20 minutes. Remove from pan and peel off paper. Let cool to room temperature.

Chocolate Tortes

Chocolate Linzer Torte

A Linzer torte is really more pie than torte. In a traditional Linzer torte, raspberry preserves are sandwiched between two layers of spiced pastry. In this recipe, a cocoa-laced spicy streusel dough is pressed into a layer pan and smeared with jam, with more pastry scattered on top. The torte needs no icing.

Makes 9 servings

¼ pound (1 stick) unsalted butter	**Pinch salt**
½ cup dark brown sugar	**1 cup cornstarch**
¼ cup cocoa, preferably Dutch-processed	**5 ounces (about 1 cup) ground walnuts**
1 teaspoon ground cinnamon	**½ cup oatmeal (not instant)**
Pinch ground cloves	**¾ cup seedless raspberry preserves**
1 tablespoon dried lemon peel	

Preheat oven to 375°F. Grease an 8- or 9-inch layer pan, line the bottom with parchment paper or foil (see page 7), grease the paper, and set aside.

In a large saucepan, melt the butter, stirring occasionally. Remove from heat and stir in the brown sugar, cocoa, cinnamon, cloves, lemon peel, salt, cornstarch, walnuts, and oatmeal until a dry, crumbly dough forms.

Press about half of the dough into the bottom of the prepared pan to form a firm, even layer. Spread the raspberry preserves evenly over the dough up to ½ inch of the edge. Break the remaining dough into small pieces and scatter evenly over the top.

Bake in the preheated oven for about 30 to 35 minutes, or until the top crust is crisp and the filling bubbles around the edge. Remove to a rack and let cool for 20 minutes. Remove from pan, remove paper or foil, and invert onto a serving plate.

Incredibly Chunky Chocolate Torte

This torte breaks all the rules I laid down earlier. The nuts are not ground, and there are as many raisins as nuts in it. The whole thing comes off as a sort of adult candy bar that can be served without glaze.

Makes 20 servings

12 tablespoons (1 ½ sticks) unsalted butter
1 ounce unsweetened chocolate, broken in half
9 ounces (1 ½ cups) semisweet chocolate chips
½ cup confectioners' sugar
3 eggs

2 tablespoons almond- or orange-flavored liqueur
2 cups pecan pieces
2 cups walnut pieces
2 cups dark raisins
2 cups golden raisins

Preheat oven to 375°F. Grease a 9-inch springform pan, line the bottom with parchment paper or foil (see page 7), grease the paper, and set aside.

In a large, heavy saucepan over medium heat, begin melting the butter. When it is half melted, add the unsweetened chocolate, remove from heat, and stir until chocolate is half melted. Add the chocolate chips and continue stirring until all the chocolate has fully melted. Mix in the sugar, eggs, liqueur, nuts, and raisins.

Pour and scrape the batter into the prepared pan and bake for 22 minutes, or until a tester inserted in the center comes out with only a moist crumb clinging to it. Do not over-bake. Cool in the pan on a rack for 20 minutes. Remove sides of springform and refrigerate torte until completely chilled, at least 3 hours.

To serve, cover with a sheet of plastic wrap and a cooling rack. Invert and remove bottom of springform pan and paper or foil. Invert serving platter onto bottom of torte. Invert torte and platter and remove plastic wrap.

Serve cool.

Fudge Torte

Don't worry if this torte seems underbaked. The fudgy pudding at its core is intentional.

Makes 10 servings

¹/₄ cup milk	3 eggs
¹/₄ pound (1 stick) unsalted butter	1 teaspoon vanilla extract
4 ounces semisweet chocolate, broken in pieces	1 ¹/₄ cups graham cracker crumbs
²/₃ cup sugar	6 ounces semisweet mini-chocolate chips

Preheat oven to 375°F. Grease an 8- or 9-inch layer pan, line the bottom with parchment paper or foil (see page 7), grease the paper, and set aside.

In a large, heavy-bottomed saucepan over medium heat, begin melting the butter. When it is half melted, add the chocolate, remove the pan from the heat when the chocolate is half melted, and stir until the butter and chocolate are completely melted. Stir in the sugar, eggs, vanilla, and graham cracker crumbs until smooth. Stir in the chocolate chips.

Pour and scrape the batter into the prepared pan and bake for 25 minutes, or until a tester inserted in the center comes out with only a moist crumb clinging to it. Do not over-bake. Cool in the pan on a rack for 20 minutes. Remove from pan and peel off paper or foil. Cool to room temperature.

One-Pot Chocolate Desserts

Chocolate Confections

Chocolate candy is unashamed. It doesn't hide within a cake or inflate itself with cream. It isn't served with a garnish or washed down with milk. Face it—it's a fix.

And it's easy. Because chocolate is a candy in and of itself, it takes very little to transform it into a distinctive confection. Simply melt it, mix it with fruit, nuts, pretzels, or spices, and set it aside to firm.

There is a hitch, though. Re-formed melted chocolate has a tendency to discolor as it cools, which creates cloudy streaks on the surface of setting chocolate. The word for these streaks is "bloom."

Bloom occurs as the melted cocoa butter in chocolate solidifies and turns into crystals as it changes from a liquid to a solid. If these crystals are allowed to develop unrestrained, they will bind together until they are large enough to become visible. Putting a few roadblocks in their way keeps the crystalline structure dispersed and thereby imperceptible.

The best way to do this is to melt chocolate used for candies in two phases. In the first step, melt about three-quarters of the chocolate. Then, away from the heat, mix in the fresh chocolate until it, too, melts. By doing so, the liquid chocolate is seeded with some of the dispersed crystals present in fresh solid chocolate. This encourages an invisible crystal structure to develop as the chocolate hardens.

Chocolate Confections

Lift dipped candies with a fork. Rap the fork against the side of the dipping bowl to help remove excess chocolate, then transfer the candy to a lined sheet pan to cool. Allow candies to set at room temperature. Avoid refrigerating chocolates; moisture from the refrigerator can cause the chocolate to become cloudy.

The other enemy of melted chocolate is moisture. Small amounts of moisture—even a drop of water—can turn a whole batch of dipping chocolate into a grainy, congealed lump. So make sure that all equipment is completely dry. Nuts should be toasted, and fresh fruit must be uncut and free of bruises or water. Naturally dry ingredients, such as pretzels, cereals, and dried fruit, can be used as they are.

Ironically, larger amounts of moisture are sometimes part of the recipe, as is the case when making fudge or soft candies. But the amount of moisture needs to be in the right proportion to the chocolate—at least 1 tablespoon of liquid to every ounce of chocolate.

By following these simple recipes, you'll find that making chocolate candies is the easiest of all chocolate work. Within minutes, you will master the techniques, and not long after, you'll be impressing everyone with your candymaking skills by turning out a wealth of chocolate-covered pretzels, chocolate-dipped chips and fruits, chocolate clusters, chocolate brittles, chocolate nut barks, and fudge.

Chocolate Porcupines

These spiny candies look like miniature porcupines, but don't let their prickly appearance intimidate you. They have the sweet and salty allure of double-dipped chocolate-covered pretzels. Chocolate Porcupines can be stored at room temperature for a day, but they should be refrigerated if you plan to keep them longer.

Makes about 30 candies

16 ounces semisweet chocolate chips   **7 ounces pretzel sticks, coarsely broken**

Place $3/4$ cup of the chocolate chips in a medium microwave-safe mixing bowl. Cover with plastic wrap and microwave at full power for 1 minute, turning once halfway through. Remove, uncover, and stir until smooth. Mix in the pretzel pieces until they are coated with chocolate.

Line a cookie sheet with wax paper or foil. Spoon the mixture onto the cookie sheet into mounds the size of rounded tablespoons. Refrigerate for at least 1 hour before dipping.

Place half of the remaining chocolate chips (about $1 1/8$ cups) in the same microwave-safe mixing bowl, cover with plastic wrap, and microwave on high for 2 minutes, turning once halfway through. Remove, uncover, and stir until smooth. Add the remaining chocolate chips and continue stirring until all the chocolate has melted.

Peel the pretzel clusters from the lined cookie sheet one at a time and drop into the dipping chocolate. Turn the clusters with a fork to ensure an even coating. Lift out the "porcupines" with the fork and slide them back onto the paper. Allow to rest until firm, about 3 hours at room temperature.

Chocolate Prunes with Almond Pits

I am a big fan of prunes and chocolate. Their shared richness, their chewy moist centers, their look-alike mahogany hues make them culinary kissing cousins. This recipe uses miniature pitted prunes (sold as "bite-sized") and replaces their pits with whole almonds. The juxtaposition of the almond crunch, the moist pillow of prune, and the hard shell of chocolate is surprising and sophisticated.

Makes 1 dozen candies

12 whole toasted almonds
12 bite-sized pitted prunes

4 ounces semisweet chocolate, broken in pieces

Press an almond into the natural indentation on the side of each prune. Mold the prune lightly around the edges of the almond. Set aside.

Melt 3 ounces of the chocolate in a covered microwave-safe bowl in a microwave oven at full power for 2 minutes, turning once halfway through. Stir to blend. Add the remaining chocolate and continue mixing until all the chocolate has completely melted. Place the prunes, one or two at a time, into the chocolate, almond side down. With a small fork, gently turn the prunes so both sides get coated.

Lift the prunes with the fork and tap on the side of the bowl, allowing excess chocolate to drip back into the bowl. Set the chocolate-dipped prunes on a sheet of foil and repeat with the remaining prunes.

Allow to set at room temperature until the chocolate coating is hard and dry, about 3 hours.

Store at room temperature or freeze for longer storage.

One-Pot Chocolate Desserts

White Chocolate Ginger Crunch

Crystallized (or candied) ginger is spicy-cool, sweet, and hot. And unlike other candied fruit-cake produce, it is neither cloying nor grainy. In this recipe, the natural complexity of the ginger is enrobed in a thick coat of white chocolate and crusted over with a crunch of nuts, a winning triumvirate.

Makes 1 dozen candies

2 ounces white chocolate, broken in pieces   **12 pieces candied (or crystallized) ginger**
$^1/_2$ to $^3/_4$ cup ground pecans or almonds

Melt the white chocolate in a covered microwave-safe bowl in a microwave oven at full power for 2 minutes, turning once halfway through. Stir.

Place the nuts on a sheet of wax paper or foil. Set aside.

Place the ginger pieces, one or two at a time, into the chocolate. With a small fork, gently turn to coat the ginger completely.

Lift with the fork and tap on the side of the bowl, allowing excess chocolate to drip back into the bowl. Set the chocolate-dipped ginger in the nuts and toss gently until well coated.

Allow to set at room temperature until the chocolate coating is hard and dry, about 3 hours.

Store at room temperature or freeze for longer storage.

Chocolate Cherry Clusters

The addition of condensed milk keeps the centers of these candies soft and creamy. The whole dried cherries and pistachios give the finished candy a bumpy casual look, but the flavor combination is anything but simple.

Makes 1 dozen candies

4 ounces milk chocolate, broken in pieces
$1/3$ cup sweetened condensed milk
$1/2$ cup dried red cherries

$1/2$ cup shelled pistachios (about 3 dozen), unsalted

    Melt the chocolate in a covered microwave-safe bowl in a microwave oven at full power for 2 minutes, turning once halfway through. Stir in the condensed milk and mix until blended. Toss in the cherries and pistachios and stir until thoroughly coated.

    Place in tablespoon-sized mounds onto a sheet of foil.

    Allow to set at room temperature until the chocolate is fully set and the candy can be easily handled, about 3 hours.

    Peel from foil and store at room temperature or freeze for longer storage.

Chewy Crunchy Chocolate Chunks

These candies are the perfect combination of my two favorite childhood treats—Rice Krispies Treats and S'mores. The warmth of the chocolate melts the marshmallows just enough to make them ooze. Stop drooling and try them for yourself!

Makes 1 dozen candies

4 ounces semisweet chocolate, broken in pieces
1 cup crisped rice cereal, such as Rice Krispies

$^1/_2$ cup mini-marshmallows

Melt 3 ounces of the chocolate in a covered microwave-safe bowl in a microwave oven at full power for 2 minutes, turning once halfway through. Stir until smooth. Add the remaining ounce of chocolate and continue stirring until all the chocolate has melted.

Stir in the cereal and the marshmallows until thoroughly coated.

Lift in tablespoon-sized mounds onto a sheet of foil.

Allow to set at room temperature until the chocolate is fully set and the candy can be easily handled, about 3 hours.

Peel from foil and store at room temperature or freeze for longer storage.

White Chocolate Almond Bark

A confession: I do not, as a rule, love white chocolate, but this candy could convert me. The slightly bitter, toasty brown quality of the almonds cuts through the cloying sweetness of the white chocolate: cream versus crunch. And this is one of the easiest candies in the world to prepare. Once the chocolate is set, just break it into shards. Don't worry if the pieces aren't all the same size and shape; a natural variety is part of this candy's charm.

Makes about 8 to 10 servings

1 cup whole almonds, skins on	**6 ounces white chocolate, broken in pieces**

Preheat oven to 400°F.

Place almonds on a sheet pan and toast them in the preheated oven until browned and crisp, about 8 minutes, stirring once.

Melt the white chocolate in a covered microwave-safe bowl in a microwave oven at full power for 2 minutes, turning once halfway through. Mix to blend. Stir in toasted almonds. Pour and scrape onto the sheet pan. Spread to an even 1/2-inch-thick rectangle. Refrigerate until firm, about 20 minutes, and break into bite-sized pieces.

Chocolate Coconut Brittle

If you swoon for chocolate-covered coconut patties, this is the candy for you. It is made in much the same way as the almond bark except that the coconut browns more quickly than the almonds, so be sure to check on it a few times and give it a simple toss to even out the browning. It is normal for coconut to toast unevenly.

Makes about 12 servings

2 cups (8 ounces) sweetened shredded coconut

8 ounces semisweet chocolate, broken in pieces

Preheat oven to 350°F.

Place the coconut on any size jellyroll pan and toast in the preheated oven until lightly browned, about 5 minutes, tossing once.

Melt 6 ounces of the chocolate in a microwave-safe bowl in a microwave oven at full power for $2^1/_2$ minutes, turning it once halfway through. Stir to blend. Add the remaining 2 ounces of chocolate and stir until it has fully melted. Stir in the toasted coconut. Pour and scrape onto the jellyroll pan. Using the back of a wooden spoon or a rubber spatula, spread into a $^1/_4$-inch-thick layer. Don't worry if there are thin spots or a few holes in the layer. Refrigerate until firm, about 10 minutes, and break into bite-sized pieces.

Bananas Foster Fudge

Fruity and intensely chocolaty, this miraculous fudge tastes as if it is permeated with sweet dark rum, even though it contains no liquor at all. The banana melts as the fudge cooks, giving the fudge a silky texture and keeping graininess to a minimum.

Makes 3 dozen pieces

1 **ripe banana, peeled**	**Pinch salt**
1 **cup dark brown sugar**	$3/4$ **cup milk**
1 **cup granulated sugar**	$1/2$ **cup ground pecans**
2 **tablespoons molasses**	3 **tablespoons unsalted butter, in pieces**
2 **ounces unsweetened chocolate, broken in pieces**	$1/2$ **teaspoon vanilla extract**

In a large, heavy saucepan, mash the banana with the back of a fork or wooden spoon. Add the sugars, molasses, chocolate, salt, and milk. Place over medium-high heat, stirring constantly, until the chocolate melts, about 3 minutes. Cover with a lid and heat until the mixture comes to a full boil, about 1 more minute.

Uncover and cook, still at a boil, until the mixture becomes shiny and thick, about 4 minutes, stirring often. When the fudge is ready, it will register 236°F to 240°F on a candy thermometer. (Or a small amount of fudge dropped into a glass of cold water will form a soft, solid wad on the bottom of the glass.) Remove from the heat and stir in the pecans.

Place the butter on the fudge and set aside to cool. When the fudge has become tepid, about 20 minutes, add the vanilla and stir until the fudge starts to firm. While still pourable, scrape into a loaf pan and set aside until the fudge is firm. Cut into 36 squares.

Hot Pepper Fudge

This cinnamon-scented fudge, with its floral scent of honey and afterglow of chile pepper, is inspired by Mexican chocolates. The flavor is most provocative when you use chipotle peppers, which are smoked jalapeños.

Makes 3 dozen pieces

2 cups sugar

2 tablespoons honey

2 ounces unsweetened chocolate, broken in
   pieces

Pinch salt

³/₄ cup milk

¹/₂ teaspoon ground chipotle pepper or
   other chile pepper

1 teaspoon ground cinnamon

3 tablespoons unsalted butter, in pieces

¹/₂ teaspoon vanilla extract

In a large, heavy saucepan, combine the sugar, honey, chocolate, salt, and milk. Place over medium-high heat, stir constantly, and heat until the chocolate melts, about 3 minutes. Cover with a lid and heat until the mixture comes to a full boil, about 1 more minute.

Uncover and cook until the mixture becomes shiny and thick, about 4 minutes, stirring often. When the fudge is ready, it will register 236°F to 240°F on a candy thermometer. (Or a small amount of fudge dropped into a glass of cold water will form a soft, solid wad on the bottom of the glass.) Remove from the heat and stir in the chipotle pepper and cinnamon.

Place the butter on the fudge and set aside to cool. When the fudge has become tepid, about 20 minutes, add the vanilla and stir until the fudge starts to firm. While still pourable, scrape into a loaf pan and even the top. Set aside until the fudge is firm. Cut into 36 squares.

Chocolate-Dipped Potato Chips

These salty-sweet confections are a cacophony of mind-boggling sensations—lean and rich, creamy and crunchy, silken and brittle. Although the notion of a chocolate-clad potato chip may seem wacky at first, you'll find these are wickedly addictive.

Makes 2 dozen to 3 dozen pieces

8 ounces semisweet chocolate, broken in pieces

2 dozen to 3 dozen thick-sliced potato chips, preferably ridged

Melt 6 ounces of the chocolate in a covered microwave-safe bowl in a microwave oven at full power for $2^{1}/_{2}$ minutes, turning once halfway through. Stir until smooth. Add the remaining 2 ounces of chocolate and stir until all the chocolate has melted.

Place the potato chips, one at a time, in the dipping chocolate. Turn to coat evenly with chocolate. Lift out with a fork. Use your thumb to help grip the chip against the fork. Shake the fork vigorously over the dipping pan to remove any excess chocolate.

Transfer to a sheet pan lined with wax paper or foil. Allow to set completely, about 1 hour, before removing from the lining.

One-Pot Chocolate Desserts

Chocolate Icings, Fillings, Glazes, and Sauces

None of the desserts in this book *requires* embellishment, but why let that stop you? When it comes to chocolate, requirements mean nothing. As with all one-pot recipes, the icings, fillings, glazes, and sauces in this chapter are made in a single vessel and are easy, foolproof, and guaranteed to reward you with a touch of extravagance in just minutes.

To ice a cake or torte, place it on a flat plate. Keep the icing off the rim of the plate by covering it with four strips of wax paper. Dip a long, cake-icing spatula into the frosting, lift out a large dollop of frosting, and spread it around the side of the cake, keeping the spatula parallel to the side. When the entire side is covered and a small rim has built up at the top of the cake, spread more frosting over the top, going all the way out to the perimeter. Finally, wipe the spatula clean, hold it parallel to the side of the cake, and turn the cake so the spatula smooths the side. Clean the spatula after each stroke. Remove wax-paper strips.

To apply a glaze to a cake or torte, set a single layer of the cake on a rack over a pan. Pour half the glaze over the top, smooth around the sides with an icing spatula or knife, pour the rest of the glaze over the top, and smooth the top. If the glaze gets too thick before you finish, warm it over low heat and continue applying it to the cake. With a large, wide spatula, transfer the cake to a serving plate.

Down and Dirty Hot Fudge Sauce

This is the perfect sauce for an instant sundae, a sliver of cake, or a quick dip for your favorite berry. It is made with defatted cocoa and just 1 tablespoon of butter, so it is surprisingly low in fat.

Makes 1 cup, or 6 servings

¹/₂ **cup cocoa powder**	¹/₂ **cup water**
³/₄ **cup sugar**	**1 tablespoon unsalted butter**
Pinch salt	¹/₄ **teaspoon vanilla extract**

In a large, heavy saucepan, combine the cocoa, sugar, and salt. Add the water and stir until smooth. Place the saucepan over medium-high heat and bring to a boil, stirring constantly.

Remove from heat and stir in the butter and vanilla until the butter is melted.

Use the sauce while still warm.

Note: This sauce can be prepared ahead, refrigerated for up to 2 weeks, and reheated over boiling water or in a microwave oven before serving.

White Chocolate Nectar

This translucent pearl-white sauce makes an extravagant dip for fresh fruit or cookies. The vanilla perfume of the chocolate is a natural enhancement to ripe peaches, bananas, and berries. You can use a different liqueur in the recipe to complement the fruit.

Makes 1 cup

²/₃ cup whole milk   4 teaspoons fruit-flavored liqueur
6 ounces white chocolate, broken in pieces

    In a heavy saucepan, bring the milk to a boil over medium heat. Add the white chocolate and stir. When the chocolate is half melted, remove from the heat and continue stirring until it is fully melted. Stir in the liqueur.

    The sauce can be served warm or at room temperature. It will become syrupy as it cools.

Chocolate Honey

The simplest of all chocolate sauces, this is an effortless opulence for gilding any plain dessert. The floral scent of honey shines through the richness of the chocolate, making it the perfect coating for a poached pear or citrus-scented tea cake.

Makes 1 cup

3 ounces semisweet chocolate, broken in pieces

$1/2$ cup honey

$1 1/2$ tablespoons brandy

Melt the chocolate and honey in a bowl set over boiling water or in a microwave oven at full power for 1 minute. Stir until smooth. Mix in the brandy until smooth.

Chocolate Sour Cream Icing

This icing appeared in One-Pot Cakes. *It is so good and so easy that I couldn't help bringing it back for an encore.*

Makes 3 cups, enough to ice 2 cake layers

12 ounces semisweet chocolate chips
1 cup sour cream, regular or low-fat (not
  fat-free)

   Melt the chocolate chips in a bowl set over boiling water or in a microwave oven at full power for 45 seconds. Stir until smooth. Mix in the sour cream until smooth.

Milk Chocolate Frosting

This is my icing of choice for a classic chocolate layer cake, served with a glass of cold milk. It is very soft and creamy and will not harden or develop a crust, even the next day—that is, if the cake lasts until the next day.

Makes 3 cups, enough to ice 2 cake layers

12 ounces milk chocolate chips
2 tablespoons unsalted butter

$^1/_2$ cup light cream

    Melt the chocolate chips and butter in a microwave oven at full power for 45 seconds or in a bowl set over boiling water. Stir until smooth. Mix in the cream until smooth.

One-Pot Chocolate Desserts

Chocolate Brandy Glaze

Use this glaze to coat any rich European-style torte or cake.

Makes ½ cup, enough to glaze a single torte

4 tablespoons unsalted butter
4 ounces semisweet chocolate, broken in
pieces

2 tablespoons brandy

In a heavy saucepan, melt the butter. Add the chocolate, reduce heat to very low, and stir until chocolate is half melted. Remove from the heat and continue stirring until the chocolate is completely melted and the glaze is smooth. Stir in brandy.

Cool before using until the glaze has the texture of heavy cream.

Brown Butter Bourbon Chocolate Glaze

The toasted flavor of browned butter gives this glaze the deep dark quality of espresso and bittersweet chocolate. It is spectacular served with cakes and tortes that contain toasted nuts.

Makes ¹/₂ cup, enough to glaze a single torte

4 tablespoons unsalted butter
4 ounces semisweet chocolate, broken in
  pieces

I tablespoon molasses
I tablespoon bourbon

In a heavy saucepan, melt the butter. Add the chocolate. Reduce heat to very low and stir until chocolate is half melted. Remove from the heat and keep stirring until glaze is smooth. Stir in the molasses and the bourbon.

Cool before using until glaze has the texture of heavy cream.

Chocolate Lekvar

Lekvar is prune butter, available in the baking section of most supermarkets. Use this sweet, fruity chocolate paste as a filling between cake layers or as a garnish for tortes and cakes that have no icing.

Makes 1 cup

4 ounces semisweet chocolate, broken in
   pieces

1 teaspoon vanilla extract

$^{1}/_{2}$ teaspoon almond extract

$^{1}/_{2}$ cup lekvar (prune butter)

    Melt the chocolate in a microwave oven at full power for 1 minute or in a bowl set over boiling water. Stir until smooth. Mix in the lekvar and the vanilla and almond extracts until smooth.

Chocolate Peanut Butter

This is a great filling for sandwich cookies made with graham crackers or plain sugar cookies. It's reminiscent of melted peanut butter cups. Spread it between the layers of a kid's birthday cake or to frost brownies, or if you're anything like me, just eat it by the spoonful.

Makes 1 1/2 cups

4 tablespoons cocoa powder
3/4 cup dark brown sugar
1/2 cup light cream
3/4 cup peanut butter, creamy or chunky

1/4 teaspoon vanilla extract
1/8 teaspoon almond extract
1 tablespoon unsalted butter

In a large, heavy saucepan, combine the cocoa and brown sugar. Add the cream and stir until smooth. Over medium heat, bring the mixture to a boil. Add the peanut butter and stir until it is half melted. Remove from the heat and stir until smooth. Mix in the vanilla and almond extracts and the butter until all are combined. Cool to room temperature.

Use as a filling or as a thick frosting for cakes.

One-Pot Chocolate Desserts

Deep Dark Chocolate Ganache

Ganache is an all-purpose chocolate filling-cum-icing that glues together the layers of a European-style pavé or enriches a sliver of torte. It is the base for most chocolate truffles, and it glazes many a petit four. This rendition is made darker and less rich by using milk instead of cream and by complementing the chocolate with a hint of honey.

Makes 1 1/2 cups

1/2 cup milk	**1 tablespoon honey**
6 ounces semisweet chocolate, broken in	**6 tablespoons unsalted butter**
pieces	**1 tablespoon brandy**

In a large, heavy saucepan, heat the milk to a boil. Add the chocolate and stir until it is half melted. Remove pan from heat and stir until the chocolate is completely melted. Add the honey and butter, and continue stirring until they are fully incorporated. Stir in the brandy.

Cool to room temperature and use as a filling or a thick frosting.

Index

C

Cake 10–19. *See also* Torte
  Applesauce Spice, Chocolate, 17
  Black and White Almond Ring, 19
  Brown Sugar, Chocolate, 10
  Buttermilk Layer, Chocolate, 12
  Carrot, Chocolate, 11
  Cherry Chocolate Swamp, 36
  Chocolate Pâté, 18
  Chocolate Rum Pudding, 37
  Chocolate Swirl Chocolate Chip
    Banana, 16
  Coffee, Chocolate Chip Marble, 15
  Orange Tea, Chocolate, 13
  Raspberry-Filled Chocolate
    Cupcakes, 14
Candy, *See* Confection
Cannoli Cheesecake, Chocolate, 35
Caramel Chocolate Flan, 40
Carrot Chocolate Cake, 11
Cheesecake, 32
  Chocolate Cannoli, 35
  Chocolate Orange Chocolate Chip, 34
  Chocolate Pudding, 39
  Very Chocolate, 33
Cherry Chocolate Clusters, 60
Cherry Chocolate Swamp Cake, 36
Chewy Brownies, Very, 26
Chewy Crunchy Chocolate Chunks, 61

chocolate
  about, 2–4. *See also* Cocoa;
  and butter, melting, 5–6
  varieties of, 3–4
Chocolate Chip
  Banana Cake, Chocolate Swirl, 16
  Bread Pudding, Triple Chocolate, 42
  Buttermilk Layer Cake, Chocolate, 12
  Cheesecake, Chocolate Orange, 34
  Chocolate Pâté, 18
  Chunky Chocolate Torte, Incredibly, 53
  Cookie Brownies, 22
  Fudge Torte, 54
  Marble Coffee Cake, 15
  Milk Chocolate Frosting, 72
  Oatmeal Raisin Brownies, 25
  Porcupines, Chocolate, 57
  Sour Cream Icing, Chocolate, 71
  Triple-X Brownies, 21
  White Chocolate Brownies, 28
  (White) Chocolate, Carrot Cake, 11
  White Chocolate Praline Torte, 50
Chunky Chocolate Torte, Incredibly, 53
citrus peel, dried, in recipes, 4
Cocoa
  Applesauce Spice Cake, Chocolate, 17
  Banana Cake, Chocolate Swirl Chocolate
    Chip, 16
  Black and White Almond Ring, 19
  Bread Pudding, Triple Chocolate, 42

Index